A
TIME
TO
GROW

By Joanne Putnam

A Time To Grow

by Joanne Putnam

©1985 Word Aflame® Press
Hazelwood, Mo. 63042

Cover Design by Tim Agnew

All Scripture quotations in this book are from the King James Version of the Bible unless otherwise identified. Some Scripture quotations from The Amplified Bible ©1965 by Zonderman Publishing House.

Printed in United States of America.

Printed by

Putnam, Joanne.
    A time to grow—.

    1. Women—Religious life. 2. Women—Conduct of life.
I. Title.
BV4527.P87   1985   284.8'43   85-20190
ISBN 0-912315-92-X

Contents

Foreword

Growth is all too often a matter taken for granted, but is actually a life-sustaining miracle of God. It is a process of change caused first by the breaking of life sustenance, and then a perpetual transformation of that original source into a mature and fruitful product.

Christ offers us life, and that more abundantly; but to claim that promise we must also learn to yield willingly to the experiences of life which cause us to embrace that life which He offers.

The weight of experience will move you as Joanne Putnam opens her heart to you in this book. As a dedicated pastor's wife, mother of three happy children, and a creative school teacher, she projects a warmth and her own special glow in revealing herself in a number of touching life-changing encounters. She is finding the secret of turning life's storms into strengths and finding the blooming cactus in the desert experiences of life.

Growth *is* possible, but not something to be taken for granted. This book will challenge you to expand yourself to reach toward those experiences in life that will bring growth in your life.

Becki Enis

Introduction

A Time To Grow. . .

We all know that growth is not an easy accomplishment. First, the seed must be planted. Then the seed must die of itself before any new life can be born and growth can begin. This seed must have a proper balance of nutrients and water before the growth can manifest itself. The dirt cannot have a high degree of acid, or the roots will be scorched. If there is too much water present, the roots will rot before they have a chance to unravel from their shell.

The seed cannot be too deeply planted, nor can it be too near the surface. It must not be in a crowded area nor in the midst of weeds or thorns. Many are the conditions of a grain of corn to produce the bountiful crop on a single stalk.

When you think of the sum total of requirements and qualifications to be met for the seed to reach a mature stage of development, it seems nearly impossible that every fall we enjoy the sumptuous taste of corn-on-the-cob with melted butter and salt! Let alone, enjoy it canned or frozen the remainder of the year!

We also know that growing physically in the human body is often quite painful. Who knows how many childhood aches and pains in legs, arms, and knees have been attributed to "growing pains." The pains are real and yet medically there is no known reason for them nor cure.

Progressing through the stages of development that enable a child to sit, crawl, walk around things, walk on his own, run, ride a bicycle, and ice skate, all involve a measure of pain at one point or another: usually at many points, unfortunately!

Needless to say, growing spiritually is also often painful. We don't like to think of it as such, but none of us are perfect creatures from the moment of our new birth. We are as newborn babies, with many growing pains ahead spiritually, and yet the painful experiences may be designed to help us become that beautiful Bride whom God is adorning.

The Book of Acts tells us that "Ye shall receive power, after that the Holy Ghost is come upon you" (Acts 1:8). Power for what? To be witnesses of course, not just verbally, but through our everyday lifestyle in our walk with God. Power to overcome the aches and pains of our spiritual growth in God so that we do not always remain in that infant state of our new birth. Paul tells us that we need to eat meat and not stay on the bottle!

At times it seems that the "pain" is unbearable. Sometimes change comes faster than we are ready for it and we stumble and fall. Occasionally our brothers and sisters, mothers or fathers in the Lord, accidentally stick us with a diaper pin as they seek to change us! It hurts, although they may not have intended to hurt us. We think, "How could they do that to me?" We could be as the little child was when his friend accidentally hurt him, he packed up his toys and went home! Later, after the growth has taken place, we are actually thankful that friends took the time and love to change our spiritual diaper, clean us up

6

a bit, and help us through a messy time in our spiritual life!

Then again, as we grow older in the Lord, perhaps the spiritual teens, we feel that we really know quite a bit. Maybe we even get a little pharisaical! We feel we need to "share" our vast amount of knowledge and wisdom with others, perhaps in the form of rebukes or "admonitions."

Hold on!

We've still got a lot of growing to do ourselves! It is only by God's unlimited grace that we have made it safely thus far!

A plant that is not nurtured will grow but not nearly as fast nor as beautifully as the one which has been given a specially prepared mixture of food. In this book, I hope to give you some food for spiritual growth. Perhaps I may present to you some areas of growth that you have not yet considered.

Many things in life can aid our growth, but we will only grow if that is our sincere desire. God will not force us to grow. We can choose at any time to stop our growth in God and become stagnant, or we can choose to forge ahead, taking one step at a time, and become the mature Christian that He delights in.

Perhaps you are a new "plant" that is just beginning to take root, or possibly you are one that is ready to shoot forth with that first most precious of blooms. Then again, maybe you are a plant that for many years has remained in the same pot. Yes, your roots are strong, but they may also be rootbound and need a little digging in the fallow ground to allow for further growth and reaching out in the Kingdom.

We are God's chosen "plants." He desires that we remain alive and healthy. Pruning is painful, but it encourages the plant to produce the healthiest vine and the most fruit. We need to be pruned. We need to be watered by the Word. There may be times when we feel we have received more water than we can handle and that we will "drown!" Just remember that God never gives us more than we can bear!

Truly growing is a tedious and lengthy process. Never forget that we serve a God who is longsuffering, and He will help us to reap a bountiful crop of the fruit of the Spirit if we will allow ourselves to be open to His guidance and instruction.

Let yourself grow
and Grow
and GROW!

1
I Am a Woman By God's Design

"And the rib, which the LORD God had taken from man, made he a woman" (Genesis 2:22).

So often, when in the world, we try to be and look like something other than who we were created to be. We are influenced by the world's fashion plates, every conceivable visual medium, and everyday peer pressure to conform to the world's standards. Whether it is makeup, cut, dyed or bleached hair, or clothing styles, we often conform. We either have an innate desire to be accepted by others or to better accept ourselves.

In working with the military, we find so many beautiful

young ladies who joined the United States Army simply to prove that they were just as good as the men! They find though, that when they come to God, and know Him in the light of His Word, that all of those former desires change. A gradual transformation begins to take place. They find out that God has not created them to be "as good as the guys" but rather to be entirely different from men! Their whole attitude about themselves change. This new awareness of who women really are gives them the confidence that they need to become the special creation God intended them to be.

When I received the Holy Ghost, many things changed in my life. The things I did, the places I went, the things I said, and the way I dressed were among the many changes. For several years I had platinum blonde hair (by no means natural). At first I didn't really think much about it, and God never did write anything in the sky concerning my hair. I hear that some people are waiting for this sort of message concerning holiness standards. It wasn't long before I heard a tug on my heart. "That is not how I made you. You are so much more beautiful to Me the way I made you." This thought pricked my heart but I continued to leave my hair as it was—platinum blonde. After all, if I dyed it back to its natural color, no one would know me and surely no one would like it, especially my fiance. It was to please him that I dyed my hair blonde in the first place! The Lord, in His longsuffering, persisted in gently dealing with me. My attitudes about many other things had changed, but I held onto that hair! It was attractive (or so I thought)! I would walk through my college campus and heads would literally turn! I was consistently reminded, "That is not how I made you!"

One day, while thinking about the Lord's soon return-ing, I realized that indeed if the Lord did come, He wouldn't know me because I was not as He had created me! That was *all* it took! What a total sense of relief I felt when I did my hair back to the original color and let it grow out naturally! I thank God that He gave me the courage to be myself.

God desires that we be our natural self and allow His precious Spirit to soften our features and take away the hard look acquired in the world. Beauticians will admit that a woman's natural hair color is much more suited to her complexion than any color which could be added or taken away. It was never God's intention that we all be made in-to artificial beauties for the world to lift up, admire and wor-ship. He does desire that we become "beautiful, radiantly beautiful" in our spirit as we grow in His Spirit.

God's primary concern is that our spirit be right. This is where He values "beauty," and from here it seeps into our whole being and overflows into the lives of others. This is why the world asks us what we "are on" or "into."

We can go through life with a facade on our soul that is seen and acknowledged by mankind, that God in a mo-ment's notice, decrees as false! This is why we need to search our souls daily, with God's insight, to see if we are really living a life pleasing unto Him. If we are not, we are fooling no one but ourselves!

If there is an area in your life that you know is not pleasing to the Lord, take it to Him. God cares for your soul. He wants to see that you grow in Him to be a vessel of honor, His spotless Bride.

There are times in our lives when we fail God. Satan desires that in these times we merely throw up our hands and quit, giving every excuse in his book as to how and why we will never make it anyway. We must always remember the Scripture in Hebrews which decrees

> *"Jesus Christ, the same yesterday, and to day, and for ever" (Hebrews 13:8).*

What a promise! He loves you just as much today, as the day He saved your soul, just as much as when you were that filthy sinner out in the world. Don't allow Satan to defeat you! Resist the devil and he will flee from you! God's love is unfathomable! The same, always and forever! Repent of your sins, faults, failures or whatever, and go on in God. Ask Him and allow Him to give you the keeping power you need to keep you from those sins, but don't quit, the time is too short.

We as wives and mothers have to be so careful that we do not become prey to Satan's trick of becoming the bearer of the "Martyr Spirit." Amidst today's fast pace and hectic schedules, we are easy prey for this trap. We are so busy that we lose sight of ourselves and our spiritual growth in God. We become so wrapped up in meeting the needs of our children and husband (and usually in this order which is clearly unscriptural) that we feel we lack the time, money, or energy to do for ourselves. This is often where Satan leaps in. We become tired, frustrated and out of touch with ourselves and God. We begin to develop negative attitudes about everything and everyone, especially ourselves. Our husbands don't understand because we don't tell them: either because we don't think they would understand or we feel they should *know* the problem without our telling them. (In other words, we expect them to be mind readers of sorts.)

Our self-esteem plummets and we fail to take care of ourselves physically or spiritually. Many women fall unconsciously in to a trap that tells them it is wrong to "love themselves," or take time for themselves.

God had to show me that to really love my husband, children, and neighbors, that I first had to love myself! He also showed me that I was teaching this concept to my children.

Occasionally we play a little game around the table at dinner time. We call it "Raise Your Hand If You Love. . ." and then we call out the names of our family members and everyone raises their hand to signify their love for that person. One night my son's name was called out and he failed to raise his hand. I asked him why he didn't raise his hand, his reply nearly tore my heart out: "You're not suppose to love yourself." That was in no wise a concept that God had instructed me to teach to my little ones! I had let negative feelings toward myself seep into his little heart. I quickly explained that God wants us to love others as we love ourselves and that he really couldn't love me or anyone else, if he didn't love himself. I thank the Lord that the next time we played the game, John David was quick to say he loved himself!

We are told today that children will progress and learn according to the rate of our expectations of them. We are no different. If we hold ourselves in low esteem, we will not be able to do anything or improve anything if we think we cannot. We have already conceded to defeat! Having an "I can with Christ" attitude means "we will with Christ" change, rearrange, or accomplish whatever we may be currently in need of.

It is important that we become aware of the person God has designed us to be, accepting who we are and trying to be as physically pleasing to God, ourselves and others as possible. God did not make us all raving beauties but He does want us to maintain a neat, godly appearance. Sometimes a woman who lacks self-esteem will confuse looking nice with worldliness. I do not believe that the Virtuous Woman of Proverbs went to the marketplace, let alone the synagogue, with tears in her dress, button facings held together by safety pins on the outside of her dress, or with bobby socks on! Solomon describes her as wearing scarlet, purple, and velvet. Clothes whose colors and fabric reflected the position of kings! Aren't we the children of a King? Find the styles and colors that are befitting to you and to God and enjoy being the special person He has created you to be!

We have all experienced things in our lives that have affected or perhaps damaged our self-image. God desires to help us to overcome these emotional scars, to heal them and to allow us to love ourselves and accept ourselves as we are designed by God Himself. Take these things to God in prayer, let Him walk through the corridors of your past and close once and for all the doors that have brought you heartache.

A positive attitude about ourselves carries over into our families. We will have a happy and contented home when we feel good about ourselves. Encourage yourself daily. Even washing dishes and changing dirty diapers can be done with a positive attitude when given to Christ. Never forget "I can do all things through Christ which strengthens me," and that strength is also our joy!

To be a happy, cheerful homemaker (notice I said

14

homemaker and not housekeeper), we must have a positive self-image. Not that we worship ourselves, God forbid, but that we realize that we have a hope!

Always remember that God Himself formed you. He accepts you as you are, and you need to accept yourself likewise. God made you, and God doesn't make junk!

2
You CAN Teach an Old Dog New Tricks

We know that every living thing traverses through processes of growth. When the growth stops, the thing dies. Our mind is a "living thing" also. It too must continue to grow or it will die! Our minds become dull, lifeless, lethargic and stale when we neglect the feeding of them. Our entire lifestyle becomes one monotonous cycle after another. We lose the zeal for living a life pleasing unto God. We slip back into things of the past because we have neglected the fresh, wholesome "food for thought" that encouraged and strengthened us in the Lord when we first began to walk with Him.

God genuinely desires that we grow. In Luke we read

about John the Baptist. Scripture decrees that he grew and waxed strong in the Spirit (which literally means, in his mental disposition). Samuel was a man of growth. We read of his childhood as he ". . .Grew on, and was in favour both with the LORD, and also with men" (I Samuel 2:26).

> *"That we henceforth be no more children, tossed to and fro, and carried about with every wind of doctrine. . .But speaking the truth in love, may grow up into him in **all things**, which is the head, even Christ" (Ephesians 4:14, 15). (Emphasis is mine.)*
>
> *"Study to shew thyself approved unto God, a workman that needeth not to be ashamed" (II Timothy 2:15).*
>
> *"Till I come, give attendance to reading, to exhortation, to doctrine" (I Timothy 4:13).*
>
> *"See then that ye walk circumspectly, not as fools, but as wise, Redeeming the time, because the days are evil" (Ephesians 5:15, 16).*

Surely our days are evil! Are you taking time to feed your mind (as a man thinketh in his heart, so is he) on material written by "evangelists, pastors, teachers" and "older women" (Ephesians 4:11 and Titus 2:3, 4). Or are you allowing the things of this world to sap you of your spiritual strength. Soap operas, women's magazines, and worldly "love" stories can never meet the spiritual needs of your life. They can only bring you down into the same situation you were in before you found the Lord.

> *"Let no man despise thy youth; but be thou*

an example of the believers, in word, in conversa-
tion [lifestyle], in charity, in spirit, in faith, in puri-
ty" (I Timothy 4:12).

What example are you setting if you set your eyes and
thoughts on things that are displeasing to Christ?

"The heart of the righteous studieth to answer"
(Proverbs 15:28).

Answer to whom? To both God and man. God in eter-
nity, man now.

"How many parents spend as much time reading as
watching television? How many go to the library as often
as the drug store? Or to the bookstore as often as the shoe
store? Not many if we believe these statistics: the average
American doesn't read one book a year, and over half the
people in the United States haven't read a book in the last
five years."*

To me this statement is incredible! I hope that we as
God's "peculiar people" have better statistics than this.
After all, we are children of the King and He does not desire
that an ignorant group of people follow Him!

"The words of the wise are as goads, and as
nails fastened by the masters of assemblies, which
are given from one shepherd" (Ecclesiastes 12:11).

Through reading, we can "hear" the words of the wise
even though we may never see or know the speaker or
writer! What an opportunity God has given us! Do you
realize that we are the only one of God's creations that can

read? Now why do you think He chose us to be very different?

It seems to me that in this day of fine Holy Ghost anointed Christian literature, that God requires more of us then simply following a Through-the-Bible-Program.

Unfortunately we are not born with complete knowledge and wisdom. Even when we are "Born into the Kingdom," we are not the possessors of a wealth of knowledge or wisdom, but we do have the potential. We, therefore, need to study. Not to show the world (though there will be times when we are sought after for answers to life's problems), but rather to be the workman that God would have us to be. Wouldn't you rather He be proud of you rather than ashamed because you have hidden the talent of learning that He so carefully designed for mankind.

We don't need to flounder and fail because we "just don't know" how to handle a problem or situation. So often the devil would have us believe that we are the only person in the entire world who has ever experienced a particular problem or gone through a similar trial. When we read the testimonies of others, we find out that indeed others have gone through something exactly like it or similar. Often we can glean from their experiences, saving ourselves immeasurable trials, and in turn, be able to share with others how to overcome similar situations in their lives.

Just because we have the Holy Ghost does not mean that our marriages are in perfect order, that our house is immaculate, that our attitude is always right or that our children are "perfect little angels!" These are things that require a considerable amount of time, wisdom, love, devotion, understanding, travail before God, common sense, and the list could go on and on! What you are able to glean from others is extremely valuable!

Today's Christain bookstores can help you. Many of them house more than books and are great sources of relaxation! (At least to me they are!) Generally speaking the clerks are very helpful and usually the books are arranged according to subject material so they are easy to locate. Clerks are usually happy to order the book or materials that you are looking for if they do not happen to have it on hand.

Granted, not every book you pick up, teaches the oneness of God, nor holds the standards that we maintain, but this is where "rightly dividing the word of truth" comes into focus. If you are solid in the knowledge of the Scriptures, have an open mind, glean and sift, you will gain much wisdom without paying quite the expense of experience you may otherwise have been required!

Some writers today go into gory details about their lives in the world. The last chapter sums it up with "Praise God, I got saved!" Stay clear of these books. They will do nothing to enhance your Christian walk.

The books I have listed in this chapter are soul enriching materials that will help you to be the woman that God requires of you. I have either read these books myself or my husband has, so I can recommend them to you with the highest of commendations. They are listed according to subject matter but of course many of them could have been cross referenced into other categories.

Please indulge yourself, and happy growth!

FOOTNOTE

How To Grow A Young Reader, A Parent's Guide to Kids and Books, by John and Kay Lindskoog.

BIBLE STUDY

Cruden's Complete Concordance. Zondervan.

Freeman, James. *Manners and Customs of the Bible.* Logos.

Halley's Bible Handbook, Zondervan.

Herr, Ethel L. *Bible Study for Busy Women.* Moody Press.

Herr, Ethel L. *Chosen Women of the Bible.* Moody Press.

La Haye, Tim, *How To Study The Bible For Yourself.* Harvest House.

Keller, W. Phillip. *A Shepherd Looks at Psalm 23.* Zondervan.

Rohn, E. *Pentecostal Home Study Course.* Pentecostal Publishing House. Word Aflame Press.

Stone, Nathan, J. *Names of God.* Moody Press.

Strong, James. *Strong's Exhaustive Concordance of the Bible.* Abingdon.

BIOGRAPHY

ten Boom, Corrie. *The Hiding Place.* Bantam.

Chalfant, William B. *Ancient Champions Of Oneness.* Pentecostal Publishing House. Word Aflame Press.

Chambers, Catherine. *The Measure Of A Man.* Pentecostal Publishing House. Word Aflame Press.

Foster, Fred. *20th Century Pentecostals.* Pentecostal Publishing House. Word Aflame Press.

Freeman, Nona. *The Adventures of Bug and Me.* Pentecostal Publishing House. Word Aflame Press.

Freeman, Nona. *Box 44, Monrovia.* Pentecostal Publishing House. Word Aflame Press.

Freeman, Nona. *Bug & Nona On the Go.* Pentecostal Publishng House. Word Aflame Press.

Landorf, Joyce. *His Stubborn Love.* Zondervan.

Landorf, Joyce. *The Richest Lady In Town.* Zondervan.

Lee, Laural. *Walking Through the Fire.* Bantam.

Reynolds, Ralph V. *Upon the Potter's Wheel.* Pentecostal Publishing House. Word Aflame Press.

Smelser, Georgia. *OMA.* Pentecostal Publishing House. Word Aflame Press.

DEPRESSION AND OVERCOMING IT

La Haye, Tim. *How To Win Over Depression.* Zondervan.

Minirth, Frank and Meier, Paul. *Happiness Is a Choice.* Baker.

Swindoll, Charles. *Encourage Me.* Multnomah Press.

Swindoll, Charles. *For Those Who Hurt.* Multnomah Press.

DOCTRINE

Graves, Robert Brent. *The God of Two Testaments.* Pentecostal Publishing House. Word Aflame Press.

Witherspoon, Jet. *Acts.* Pentecostal Publishing House. Word Aflame Press.

FICTION

Andrews, Gini. *Esther–The Star and the Sceptre,* Zondervan.

Henderson, Lois, *Hagar–A Novel.* Christian Herald.

Henderson, Lois. *Ruth–A Novel.* Christian Herald.

Holmes, Marjorie. *Two From Galilee.* Bantam.

Landorf, Joyce. *Joseph.* Revell.

Marshall, Catherine. *Christy.* Avon.

Oke, Janette. *Love Comes Softly.* Bethany House Publications.

Oke, Janette. *Love's Enduring Promise.* Bethany House Publications.

Oke, Janette. *Once Upon a Summer.* Bethany House Publications.

Sheldon, Charles. *In His Steps.* Zondervan.

Traylor, Ellen Gunderson. *Song of Abraham.* Living Books.

GENERAL INTEREST

Capps, Charles. *The Tongue–A Creative Force.* Harrison House.

Kilgo, Edith. *Money in the Cookie Jar.* Baker Bookhouse.

Kilgo, Edith. *Money Management: Dollars and Sense for Christian Homemakers.* Baker Book House.

Kirby, Scott. *Dating.* Baker Book House.

Lockervie, Jeanette. *Salt In My Kitchen.* Moody Press.

Mandino, Og. *The Greatest Salesman In The World.* Bantam Books.

Petty, Jo. Compiler. *Apples of Gold.* C. R. Gibson Co.

Petty, Jo. Compiler. *Wings of Silver.* C. R. Gibson Co.

Reeves, Kenneth V. *The Angels, Demons and People.* Pentecostal Publishing House. Word Aflame Press.

Schnell, William. *30 Years a Watch Tower Slave.* Baker Book House.

Swindoll, Charles. *Hand Me Another Brick.* Bantam Books.

HEALTH

Brand, Paul and Yancy, Philip. *Fearfully and Wonderfully Made.* Zondervan.

Coyle, Neva. *Free To Be Thin.* Bethany.

Hunter, Frances. *God's Answer to Fat. . .Loose It!.* Hunter Ministries.

McMillan, E. I. *None of These Diseases.* Revell.

MARRIAGE AND FAMILY

Adams, Joy E. *Marriage, Divorce & Remarriage.* Baker Book House.

Campbell, Ross. *How To Really Love Your Child.* Victor Books. SP Publications.

Dillow, Linda. *Creative Counterpart.* NT.

Dobson, James. *Dare To Discipline.* Bantam Books.

Dobson, James. *Hide Or Seek.* Revell.

Dobson, James. *Straight Talk To Men And Their Wives.* Word.

Dobson, James. *What Wives Wish Their Husbands Knew About Women.* Tyndale.

Herdebrecht, Paul. *Fathering a Son.* Moody Press.
La Haye, Tim. *How To Be Happy Though Married.* Tyndale.
La Haye, Tim and Beverly. *The Act of Marriage.* Zondervan.
Narramore, Bruce. *Why Children Misbehave.* Zondervan.
Swindoll, Charles. *Strike The Original Match.* Multinomah Press.

MEN

Getz, Gene. *Measure Of A Man.* Regal.
Now remember this is a woman's book! Certainly there are many good books for men in the MARRIAGE AND FAMILY SECTION!

TIME MANAGEMENT

Dillow, Linda. *Priority Planner.* NT.
Miller, Ruth. *The Time Minder.* Christian Herald.
Young, Pam and Jones, Peggy. *Sidetracked Home Executives.* Warner Books.

WOMEN

Bouma, Mary La Grand. *The Creative Homemaker.* Bethany Fellowship.
Bush, Barbara. *A Woman's Workshop on Mastering Motherhood.* Zondervan.
Dobson, James. *Prescription For A Tired Housewife.* Tyndale.
Getz, Gene. *Measure Of A Woman.* Regal.
Haney, Joy. *The Privileged Woman.* Pentecostal Publishing House. Word Aflame Press.
Haney, Joy. *The Radiant Woman.* Christian Life Press.
Hanford, Elizabeth. *Me? Obey Him?* Sword of the Lord Publications.
Hanford, Elizabeth. *Your Clothes Say It For You.* Sword of the Lord Publications.
La Haye, Beverly. *Spirit–Controlled Woman.* Harvest House.

Morgan, Nell and Chambers, Catherine. *Preserving the Pentecostal Lady.* Pentecostal Publishing House. Word Aflame Press.

Ortlund, Anne. *Disciplines of the Beautiful Woman.* Word.

Owens, Pat. *Idea Book For Mothers.* Tyndale.

Pentecost, Dorothy Harrison. *The Pastor's Wife and the Church.* Moody Press.

Pippert, Rebecca M. *Out of the Saltshaker.* Inter-Varsity Press.

Rockness, Miriam Hoffman. *Keep These Things—Ponder Them In Your Heart—Reflections of a Mother.* Tyndale.

Segraves, Daniel L. *Women's Hair.* Pentecostal Publishing House. Word Aflame Press.

Wallace, Mary H. *My Name Is Christian Woman.* Pentecostal Publishing House. Word Aflame Press.

Wallace, Mary. *Pioneer Pentecostal Women.* Pentecostal Publishing House. Word Aflame Press.

Wallace, Mary. *Pioneer Pentecostal Women II.* Pentecostal Publishing House. Word Aflame Press.

Wilkerson, Gwen, and Schonauer, Betty. *In His Strength.* Regal Books.

All of the above books can be ordered from Pentecostal Publishing House, 8855 Dunn Rd., Hazelwood, Mo. 63042.

By no means is this the entire list of good books available today. These are but a few that have been instrumental to me. I admonish you to do some reading if you are not already. Read the Word, read about the lives of great people, and read books that have been instrumental in changing attitudes that promote scriptural principles.

There is a familiar old saying that states, "You should learn something new everyday." What a better way to learn some new tricks!

3

Thou Art Come To The Kingdom For Such A Time As This

"And who knoweth whether thou art come to the kingdom for such a time as this?" (Esther 4:14).

So often today, we hear people speak of "the good ole days" when people were friendly, a dollar was worth something and there was a sense of morality still being exhibited. People remark that they wish they lived "back then." It is ironic, therefore, to find that nearly 3,000 years ago, Solomon wrote

> *"Say not thou, What is the cause that the former days were better than these? for thou dost not inquire wisely concerning this"* (Ecclesiastes 7:10).

People really haven't changed much have they?
As children of God, we realize that as Ecclesiastes declares

> *"To every thing there is a season, and a time to every purpose under the heaven: A time to be born, and a time to die"* (Ecclesiastes 3:1-2).

David of old said

> *"I will praise thee; for I am fearfully and wonderfully made: marvellous are thy works; and that my soul knoweth right well. My substance was not hid from thee, when I was made in secret"* (Psalm 139:14, 15).

And we, as David were created by God. He knew us before we existed! God indeed chose our time to be born.
Isaiah told us in his book, chapter 46:10 that God knows our lives, He knows the end from the very beginning! God knew what we would look like, what our name would be, where we would be born, how many hairs there would be on our head, literally everything about us! He knew everything about us from that split second of our creation in conception! He knew what our lives would hold, our husband, children, hopes, dreams, even our eternal destiny.

In essence, what was said of Esther can be said of you and me—"We are come to the kingdom for such a time as this."

I would like to address your "time" as a wife today. If you believe Ecclesiastes 3:1, 2 to be an accurate account of God's foreknowledge, then you would agree that God knew ages ago who would marry and all of the what, when, where and whys about your marriage. He also knew what *could* and *would* become of your marriage.

Often people become confused in the area of "would" and "could" become. Many think that God has predestined our lives and that it does not really matter what we do, it will become as God has ordained it. Not so my friend!

"For whom he did foreknow, he also did predestinate to be conformed to the image of his Son, that he might be the firstborn among many brethren" (Romans 8:29).

God has predestinated us to become His children but He will never force us into that subjection. If we *do* allow ourselves to be born into His kingdom, then we are comfortable with the future that God has ordained for us.

If you are a child of God then you can willingly accept the fact that you are in the Kingdom of God at this particular time and place for His glory. You also accept the fact that the husband you have has been given to you. That you are bone of his bone and flesh of his flesh as the Scriptures declare you to be.

How is your relationship with that man whom God has given to you?

What if your husband became famous some day, a

great and notable man? You have probably heard the old saying "Behind every great man is a great woman." Have you ever thought what might be said of you?

"She nagged and pushed until he made it to the top."

"She used her position, influence and coersion to get him to the top."

"She loved and encouraged him, uplifted him, took time to listen to him, let him express his frustrations without being critical and she tried to understand him and help him understand himself."

Are we like Job's wife? When the pressures mount and failure seems eminent, do we reach a breaking point and tell our husband to "curse God and die!" Or do we hang on, seek God with our husband, and try to build up his faith with words of encouragement? We need to let him know that though we have lost something physical (perhaps a job in this time of uncertain employment), we have not lost the spiritual.

Are we like Sarah, who knew the promise of God but didn't have the faith or the patience to wait on God? She decided to take things into her own hands (perhaps like the wife who is trying to push her husband into the ministry) and probably nagged, pleaded, begged and pouted until Abraham followed her leading in taking Hagar as his concubine—a decision she sorely regretted in the ensuing years.

Are we like Rebekah who also knowing the promise of God, used her "favorite" son to deceive her almost blind husband to make sure it "came to pass?"

Are we like Abraham Lincoln's wife who was known to throw a cup of hot coffee in his face amidst a large boarding house dining room?

Are we like the woman of today who for many years scraped and saved to purchase a fine set of china, beautiful silver and elegant crystal for those "special" occasions, then upon her husband's sudden and unexpected death, she realized that the most important person in the world to her had never eaten one meal from the fine china, never taken one bite with the beautiful silver, nor had taken one sip from the elegant crystal.

Are we always complaining, always criticizing? Are we never satisfied with our husband? Assuring him that he does nothing right. Reminding him that he's too tall or too short or too fat or too thin? He walks crooked, his ears stick out, he doesn't match his clothes well, he never makes enough money, never does enough around the house. . . .

Or do we strive to be as the virtuous woman of Proverbs who is the wife God indeed intended her to be?

> *"A virtuous woman is a crown to her husband: but she that maketh ashamed is as rottenness in his bones" (Proverbs 12:4). (Reminds me of cancer!)*
>
> *"Every wise woman buildeth her house: but the foolish plucketh it down with her hands" (Proverbs 14:1). (More often than not, with her mouth!).*

According to Scripture, we need to be reverencing our husbands as Paul tells us to in Ephesians 5:33. The *Amplified Version* of this Scripture, states: "And let the wife see that she notices him, regards him, honors him, prefers him, venerates and esteems him, defers to, praises him, loves him, admires him, exceedingly!"

31

If we break that down it looks like this:

She notices him

Pays attention to him, notices when he comes home, welcomes him royally into the home that he provides for the family, doesn't treat him like a piece of furniture that is old and haggard.

She regards him

Takes special pleasure in him, his looks and his needs. Takes a special pride in his clothes looking neat, clean and well-pressed. (Ouch, that stepped on a few toes.)

She prefers him

To desire his company above anyone else's and tell him so.

She venerates and esteems him

To lift him up, to give herself wholeheartedly to him, to have a high regard for him, he should be her number one person!

She defers to

Asks him his preference and does not pout because she really wants her own way. (I hear you Lord!)

She praises him

To be affectionate towards him, *tell* him what he does well, and soon the things he doesn't do so well, will probably improve!

She loves him

Directs her attention to him. (Remember that you were

first a wife and then a mother. Don't get your priorities mixed up in this area.)

She honors him

Believe it or not this literally means to worship and pay honor to him. Sara called Abraham Lord!

She admires him

EXCEEDINGLY!

"Oh, but you don't know *my* husband!" You're right, I don't, but God does, and He said that He would never give you more than you can bear. Do you really trust Him, even with an unsaved husband?

If you desire to be all that God would have you be, then allow Him to work through you to be the wife that He desires you to be in these crucial last days.

You, as Esther, have come to the kingdom for such a time as this. Allow God to use you to save your family as He allowed Esther to save her people!

4

Our Precious Heritage

"Lo, children are an heritage of the LORD: and the fruit of the womb is his reward" (Psalm 127:3).

*T*hink of it, "an heritage of the LORD!" And what do we do with "an heritage?" If it were an expensive vase or elaborate oil painting, we would find a safe place to keep it. We would lovingly and painstakingly protect it, keeping it from any impending or unforeseen danger. How much greater is the "living" heritage God has placed within our care!

Past history tells us of the shame and degradation

brought upon women who were unable to bear children. It was considered a curse from the Almighty God to be barren, and yet modern society has almost led us to believe that the opposite is true today!

We find, often to our dismay, that the little round bundle of joy that arrives after a long anticipated period of time, is demanding, self-centered, much too vocal, and at times, quite arrogant! Many women find themselves in a literal state of shock and are unable to cope with even the most minimal of tasks in the baby care. The term used today is "Baby Blues." Diapers, feeding on demand, soured milk and sudden total disruption of the norm, are not what they thought they were getting! They no longer recall the moments of sanctified prayer for their yet unborn babe and they fail to draw from the promises that God has so graciously given us. The first promise may very well be that He would never give us more than we could bear!

We, as adults, lose sight of childhood at an amazingly accelerated pace as we grow older. We forget the frustrations, feelings of inadequacies, and intense need of physical as well as emotional love that encompasses a child. We forget the joy of the outdoors and the many "worlds" to explore there, desperately we try to dissuade their explorations of eating dirt and climbing trees! In jest we cajole our children to find that we are in essence actually provoking them to wrath. We demand apologies and explanations from them, that we, as their prime examples, are unwilling to give.

God has given us an immense responsibility along with His inheritance. We are instructed to train our children in the way they should go, to teach them diligently about the one true God. We are to love them, discipline them, provide for them, to nurture and control them. In doing so, He has given us promises concerning them, in that, if we obey Him in being all He desires us to be as parents, we will experience the blessings of joy and satisfaction that nothing else could ever give us.

Truly when God gives us a baby, He gives us a hidden treasure chest! A beautiful inheritance with promise! Inside this treasure chest, are many delicately wrapped treasures and talents. Some are precious jewels that once seen or touched, vanish into nothingness. And yet we do not sorrow, for that is part of the rare beauty of it. Some are permanent, but change is ever present. Every treasure is pliable, and is molded by its environment. They can be allowed to flourish into limitless beauty or be pressed into unnatural submission that destroys their very essence.

Some of these precious gifts are never seen by the human eye, but the touch is nonetheless felt with great intensity. Indeed, along the course of life, there are also painful ones, but often they are the ones which spark us to grow and be stronger in God.

These precious treasures remind me of the delicate, rich, soft colors of thread that are woven into the magnificent Persian rugs of the Orient. The most expensive and intricately woven are said to be one of a kind, as is that special inheritance that God has given to us. As the "threads" of a child's life are woven together, they produce a priceless tapestry called "Life." The excellence of this tapestry is determined by the quality of the materials used in the "loom," and the "care" taken in forming the design.

It is extremely important how these fine threads are woven into the tapestry. They must be handled carefully, considerately, and with love and tenderness. Yet they need to be reinforced with threads of discipline in order to develop a sturdiness and stability.

We must ever be mindful that the design which we have chosen for the tapestry, may not be what the master designer desires. We must be cautious never to weave the tapestry into what we would have woven for ourselves, had we held the spindle of our own life in our hands.

God gives us the life, and the life has many properties that we can and cannot change. But we are *only* the weaver who moves the shuttle in and out of the "warp" that God has fashioned. We must be in constant communication with Him, to be assured that we form the desired arrangement.

God has given us, as mothers, an extremely important and indeed awesome task. It is one that He felt was within our capabilities if we but allow Him to be our constant guide and resource person.

It is my desire to stand before the Throne of Grace one day and have it said of me

> *"And he lifted up his eyes, and saw the woman and the children; and said, Who are those with thee? And [she] said, The children which God hath graciously given thy servant"* (Genesis 33:5 made personal).

5

Capture Your Vapor

"For what is your life? It is even a vapour, that appeareth for a little time, and then vanisheth away" (James 4:14).

We know assuredly that this Scripture is true. Our lifespan, be it seventy, eighty, or ninety years, when compared to the eons of time, is just like the steam that billows from your teapot! You see it for a few short seconds and then it is gone, never to be seen, felt or heard again. Experience has shown us that when we harness this elusive substance, we are able to maneuver large steamships, power great locomotives and heat huge buildings with relatively little effort. This steam, or vapour, when harnessed, holds untold power. Our lives can be just as powerful if we "harness" them, or put our lives in order to make them work for us.

Such a simple thing as writing, can be just what we need to put our lives in order. If we take time to sit down and plan, organize, budget, schedule, set goals, set priorities and put down our thoughts, we will be putting that vapor of our lives into a constructive force that is capable of changing lives, namely our own!

I can hear you now, "Oh, but I can't write," or "That sounds like too much work for me," or "I wouldn't have any idea where to begin." Remember, we are talking about growth!

Job 10:22 tells us that in darkness there is no order. We are children of the light, therefore, we need order in our lives, not the chaos that darkness brings. You've been in a darkroom before. Things are unclear and you stumble over things and are unable to find what you need. Turning on even the smallest light makes all of the difference.

I Corinthians 14:40 admonishes us to, "Let all things be done decently and in order." Looks like we can't escape it!

God has a specific order in all that He does. A look into the first chapter of Genesis on the days of creation, gives you a complete view of the preciseness of His order. We even read about His premeditation concerning the creation of man. I don't believe He needed to write all of the details on paper in order to remember them (as I always have to do) but He could have!

We wouldn't think of building a new home without making a very precise blueprint of every minute detail involved, material needed, cost estimated and scheduled date of completion before that first shovelful of dirt is dug for the foundation. Why then, do we build our lives any differently? Why do we build them so haphazardly? As the old saying goes, "If you fail to plan, you plan to fail."

I have found that the only way for me to bring order to my life, is to sit down with a paper and pen and "order it!" Somehow it always seems things get put together faster, easier and more precisely when I put it in writing first. A little premeditated thought can save a lot of time, energy and effort.

This writing can take on many forms. For you it may begin with making up lists. "I do make up lists," I hear you say. But what do you do with them after you make them up? Can you even remember where you put them and whether you wrote it on the back of an envelope, on a partially used napkin or on the scrap of brown paper bag you tore off in a hurry? If you do make up lists, begin with having a convenient place or container to keep them in.

How many times have you spent the entire day running to and fro, trying to accomplish everything in one day, only to find out that you either did a considerable amount of backtracking, forgot half of the things you needed to get, or totally forgot the most important item of the day? Frustrating wasn't it? It doesn't have to be!

Sit down. (Make the time.) List all you need to do and where. Then decide what your priorities are. What needs to be done first, second, third. Keep your plan intact. Take it with you and accomplish all you set out to do.

Actually this can only be the beginning of getting your life ordered. For me, this type of writing developed into setting spiritual goals and recording the progress I made.

41

It provided for me, a sense of release that no other medium could do as effectively.

Writing became for me, sort of a silent friend that could sort out my fears and frustrations. Writing them down helped me to look at my fears and frustrations objectively and overcome them easier. I'll never forget an extremely frustrating time in my life. My notes for that day began, "A year ago today, I could truthfully say, I don't know how any woman with the Holy Ghost could have a nervous breakdown. Today I can't say that because I know how close I came to having one. . . ."

At the time it was not funny. Today it sort of is because I know that by releasing those feelings on a piece of paper rather than on my husband, I was able to get control of my emotions which were running wildly. I was also able to reevaluate some things and get my priorities in line again, without too much strain on my husband!

Today, I find preserving memories to be one of my most favorite reasons to write. Seeing the dates my children accomplished certain feats and what and how they said and did things, makes the little time I spent jotting them down well worthwhile. Notes like: "Amy told us her Sunday school lesson was 'bout Madam and Even in the garden. The teacher read her the scriptions about them. She said they also talked about Moseph." and "May 8, 1979. Teaching John David to go down steps—can go down fine but begins head first!" and "John woke up sick last night and wanted to know why—he figured I was expecting again. He was right!" I read about one mother that had kept spiral notebooks, one for each year, and recorded all of the family events, birthdays, and holidays throughout her marriage. What a treasure as the children grew older, and returned to sit by the fire as the mother related the many incidents that would otherwise have been totally forgotten.

Another avenue of writing that I have thoroughly enjoyed is that of writing out my prayers. There is something special about having something written with the date and seeing how quickly He brings it to pass. I had been praying for nearly twelve years that my mother would be filled with the Holy Ghost. It wasn't two weeks after I wrote it down with my prayer requests that indeed she had received the Holy Ghost! Believe me, there was no magic in the fact that I had just written it down, but it was fantastic anyway!

I've also enjoyed praying through the Word much like David did in the Psalms.

> "Lord let *my* delight be in Thy law, let *me* meditate on it day and night. Let *me* be like a tree that's planted by the rivers, that bringeth forth fruit in his season, don't let me faint or wither. Thou oh Lord, art a shield for me. My glory, and the uplifter of my soul. Oh Lord, how excellent is Thy name!"

Praying the Word is exciting! It makes the Bible very personal, just as God desires that it be to us. God's promises can become tailor fitted when we pray in this fashion, also we begin to become more clearly aware that God's promises require something of us before we can receive them, something we all too soon forget!

Recording the many, both large and small, miracles that God so graciously grants us is another item that deserves attention. God has done so many special things for me: saving my mother, allowing my freezer to go out the week before the guarantee ran out, and allowing some dear soul to leave a short stubby pencil behind to entertain my little one! God is so good and we need to be reminded of it from time to time!

It doesn't even hurt to write down special compliments that have been given to you. My favorite one came from my husband (of course!). He had aspirations of becoming President before he found the Lord and when he gave me the following compliment one day, I took it as a very high honor: "Hon, you would have made a good President's wife!"

Who can write? Everyone! Especially you! Forget the grades you had in English class in composition or handwriting. Look at it as a way of expressing your vapor, harnessing it and putting it to use for you, as only you can.

One of the nicest things about writing is that it is not an expensive hobby and yet it can be one of the most pleasurable experiences, and profitable, that you have ever encountered (outside of the Lord of course). If you do choose to do some writing, all you really need is a pen or pencil and paper. A special treat is in using a real fountain pen. There is just something special about a *real* fountain pen! The paper need not be special though I would advise you to use a notebook of some sort to maintain that ordered effect. I prefer a looseleaf notebook because I like to move things around and I don't like to tear things out of a spiral notebook. If you really want to get into this you can purchase fine vellum stationery and a handtooled leather notebook, but none of this is really necessary!

Whatever you do, try to keep your notes together and

date each one of them. I have many notes and poems from my early years that have no date on them and are written on every type of paper imaginable. Quite frustrating to say the least! Also, remember, if you find a poem or thought that someone else has written, be careful to give them the credit for it. Some of the things I so carefully preserved, I'm not really sure I wrote!

Keeping a journal is an interesting endeavor. It need not be something that forces you to write some trivial bit of information in each day. It can be a special place where you write your thoughts for God alone to read, or it could be like mine, a compendium of thoughts, prayers, reflections. . . . In many ways my journal reflects my growth or lack of it in particular areas.

Capture your "vapor." It can help you to establish hopes and dreams, set priorities in your life and give you the order that your soul desires. Where would we be today if Matthew, Mark, Luke and John had not captured the vapor of our Lord's life for us to know who He really was?

6
On Becoming
The Virtuous Woman!

*F*or most Christian women, the virtuous woman of Proverbs 31 is their ideal. She is the epitome of "Christlikeness" in a woman. Today we would call her a "superwoman!"

Some women probably wish they had never found her! They feel they do their best and regret the fact that scripturally there is someone they need to align themselves with! It reminds me of my Aunt Martha who never wanted to learn how to milk the cow, for she knew that if she learned, she would probably have the task assigned to her permanently!

When taking a look through Proverbs 31 beginning

with verse 10 we find that the virtuous woman exhibits these qualities or talents:

1. Her husband trusts her. She does what she says. She doesn't do anything that could be harmful to him or her family. She probably keeps things somewhat to herself and certainly doesn't spread the family problems around the neighborhood.

2. She will do him good and not evil all the days of her life. Those vows she took on her wedding day were more than just passing words.

3. She enjoys making things with her hands.

4. She's thrifty, looks for the best prices, probably uses cents off coupons and watches for seasonal sales!

5. She is not slothful; she doesn't sleep late in the morning; she gets up and cooks her family a good nutritious meal before they go off to work or school. She plans her menus ahead of time to make sure that she has everything on hand when she begins to prepare something. None of that "hurry, run to the store, I need something" for her.

6. She is capable of buying land or running a business at home, making it profitable for her to remain at home if she so desires.

7. She is industrious. She makes a product that is top quality. She has too many orders for her merchandise because it is so good!

8. She's not selfish. She takes time to help others and does it in a loving spirit. She has learned the principle of casting her bread upon the waters.

9. She makes sure her family is well clothed yet she doesn't spend a fortune on it. Through watching sales, frequenting thrift shops and yard sales, and sewing, others think her husband's entire paycheck goes for clothes!

10. She may make her own clothes or purchase them, but they are never shabby. She remembers who her heavenly Father is and desires to be a good reflection and witness for Him.

11. She openeth her mouth with wisdom; and in her tongue is the law of kindness. Advice is never given in the "Well, if I were you. . . ." When she does give advice, it is with wisdom and never with cutting sarcasm or "I told you so."

12. She looks well to the ways of *her* household. She is not trying to run everyone else's. She doesn't idle the day away then at night discover that she has accomplished absolutely nothing.

What is it all worth? Her husband praises her and her children love her. Even her community (friends, family, associates) admires the family because of her virtuous acts. You certainly could not hire such work done for a few rubies!

Several years ago, some of the popular women's magazines tried to put a price tag on the individual jobs and responsibilities that today's women have. They came up with a minimum salary that would average $25,000 yearly! Yet as Christian mothers, we have an even greater responsibility to our families. Certainly no one can put a price tag on the love of Christ that we are to transmit to our loved ones.

At times we may feel like we are commensurate with

this virtuous woman. We feel we're on top of everything. After all we don't have three baskets of ironing lurking in some closet, and we are not attacked by an avalanche when we open a cupboard. We feel we are meeting the needs of our husband and children and meeting our spiritual goals. No easy task, whether we have an outside job or not.

At other times we feel like—WOW! How did that woman in Proverbs ever do it? She didn't have a washer, dryer, stove, refrigerator, blender, mixer, toaster, microwave, sewing machine, or Roto-tiller. She did not even have hot and cold running water!

Most of us at one time or another have worked outside the home. Some of us have felt that when we did so, we were more organized and better able to "stay on top of things." It seemed that we usually tried harder to make better use of our time, and to schedule our time so that it worked *for* us and not *against* us. It seems that when we are home all of the time—all schedules disintegrate! Whether it be our failure to make or keep a schedule, or there are so many outside interruptions, that we completely forget about planning a schedule.

There is a principle that explains it quite well. Parkinson's Law states: "Work expands to fill the time available for its completion." (We all knew this was true; we just never took the time to write it down!) Consequently if we fail to schedule a time or date of completion for any task or project, we will allow it to drag on and on and perhaps never really complete it! Surely you have been in homes where remodeling has begun, if no date of completion is set, you may return ten years later to find that there is still no linoleum on the kitchen floor! This was not due to the lack of funds, but rather lack of time (scheduled time that is!)

As I mentioned in "Capture Your Vapor" God desires our lives to be organized. Chaos and disorder have never been God's attributes and certainly He does not desire that His children let chaos envelope their lives.

We find in Ecclesiastes 5:1 - 12, quite an exhortation concerning time. I find verse eighteen especially interesting; "And also that every man [or woman in our case] should eat and drink, and enjoy the good of all his [her] labour, it is the gift of God." (Author's paraphrase.)

How often have we grumbled and complained because we have so much "to do"? This is *not* God's perfect will for our lives. If we can develop a schedule, stick to it, and organize our home so we run it instead of it running over us, we *will* be able to "enjoy the good of all our labour." I know because I've experienced it!

Organization and cleaning have never been a "highpoint" in my life. As a matter of fact during my college days I lived with my grandmother. My room was upstairs and out of the mainstream of visitors, so I had very little "outside" motivation to keep it in order. My fiance (who is now my husband) was there one day while I was in school. He was working on a drawing and needed a ruler. Grandma sent him to my room and told him surely I had one on my desk. After several minutes, my grandmother became concerned when he didn't return immediately. She called to him and asked if he hadn't found the ruler yet. His reply was, "I haven't found her desk yet, let alone the ruler!"

We've been married several years now and if he complains about something awry, I remind him that he knew how I was before he married me and how the Lord has helped me to make a miraculous improvement since then! He has to agree.

Our home is to be our "heaven on earth." We need to keep our homes pleasing as unto the Lord. If your husband is like mine, he cannot stand clutter. Clutter really doesn't bother me, but because I know that it annoys him, I try to keep it under control. No easy task with three little ones, but it is possible!

Your home does not have to be a "House Beautiful" front cover photo, but neither should it be a pigpen. This often quoted "scripture": "Cleanliness is next to godliness," is *not* in the Bible, but it does have a considerable amount of merit!

A lady came to visit one evening and asked me to share my little organizational scheme with her. She was desperate; she had absolutely no motivation to clean anything at any time. It was so bad that her husband would not allow her to use real plates any longer because they never got washed unless he did it! She was more or less asking me to show her some magic formula for keeping the house clean, clothes washed and ironed, family fed, errands ran, closets clean and shopping done without lifting a finger! That is by no means what I have to share with you! As far as I know, such a system doesn't exist unless it is called "Rent-a-maid!"

To accomplish the many tasks involved in running an efficient home, even to sufficiently begin, you must have a sincere desire to do so, and be willing to discipline yourself. Without the desire and discipline, you will remain in the state you are in.

Today there are many books on the secular and

religious market that, if adhered to, could effectively help you "set your house in order." A key to becoming that virtuous woman. Refer to the Chapter "You Can Teach an Old Dog New Tricks" if you would like to read further into time management principles concerning your home. A visit to the local library could be very enlightening in this area.

The book that really "ministered" to me in this area was: *Sidetracked Home Executives, S.H.E.* It was written by Pam Young and Peggy Jones, two sisters, who became absolutely desperate due to no control or organization in their homes. They were known to greet their husbands at the door when they returned from work, wearing their unchanged nightclothes! Through desperation and much prayer, they developed a system to help themselves correct their motives, clean and organize their homes and effectively share it with others to help them get out of the mess they found themselves in.

They have developed an organizational card file system which I would like to share briefly with you. It is one that emphasizes a positive attitude, does not expect overnight success and is achievable. To set this program in motion, they suggest you use either a 3 x 5 or 4 x 6 card file box and cards. (I've chosen a 3 x 5 plastic file box that is twice as deep as normal). They also suggest that instead of the traditional white cards, that you choose colored cards. Each card represents a particular sequence of doing chores: yellow for daily chores, blue for weekly tasks, white for monthly and seasonal projects and pink for personal and errands. These can be readily obtained from an office supply store and are usually not any more expensive than white ones.

You will also need tabbed index cards that are numbered from 1 - 31. These will serve as your days in the month. After you have purchased your card file box, find a small calendar for the entire year, and tape it to the inside of the lid of your box. (Quite a time saver when you are trying to organize large blocks of time, with a quick glance you can see the entire year.)

You will also need two sets of alphabetically tabbed index cards and a set of tabbed index cards that you can use for special sections. It is suggested that you include in this file, your traditional "phone book." Putting one name and address on each card, plus pertinent information concerning that person or family; birthdays, anniversaries, preferences, ages, sizes, likes, dislikes. The second set of ABC cards are used to file information, location of items and special notes. I'll mention more later on this subject. The blank cards should be labeled with headings such as the following: Weekly, Improvements, Monthly, Special, Gifts, Mini-jobs, Storage, Twice yearly, Miscellaneous, and other catagories you may find that are appropriate to meet your needs. Remember you are not bound by my suggestions nor the book's. Each woman has different needs in these areas according to her home and duties.

One of the most important aspects of this system is to make sure you are up one half hour before the rest of the mainstream of your family. How you use this time is entirely up to you, but I prefer devotional time. For some totally unknown reason, it seems that everyone else gets up in a better mood when I've had a talk with the Lord first! (Wonder why?)

Another crucial point is having a plan for each day and each week, plus a skeleton plan for the month. You will find if you take time to plan, that you will have deserved free time to do things that you enjoy doing, plus you will feel so much better about yourself, your family and the Lord. Remember what Ecclesiastes 5:13 said?

Some very pertinent sugggestions are:

1. Don't have an "anytime" routine.
2. Never leave the house before you have done *all* of the morning's daily chores.
3. Check the next day's schedule the night before.
4. Don't overlook yourself.
5. Refile your cards as you complete them.

The book suggests that you go to each room of your house or apartment with a paper and pencil. Make a list of *every possible* job to be done in that room. (Dust, sweep, mop, wash walls, windows, mirrors.) Also note the amount of time it would take you to complete the task (be realistic) and how often you do it, or rather *should* do it. Often when we realistically evaluate ourselves, we find that perhaps we do some things more frequently than we should and others not as frequently as we should because it isn't our favorite thing to do. Perhaps it is a game that should be delegated to someone else. Decide how often it needs to be done, daily, weekly, monthly, semi-annually, annually. Do this in every room or area of your home.

Now transfer each item to the corresponding card (if using the color-coded cards). Record the job, approximate time involved to complete it and if it is daily, every-other-day, or weekly. If it is a job which takes less than ten minutes to complete, then it is considered a mini-job and can be done at odd spare minutes, perhaps while you are talking on the phone or if the work is portable, when you are waiting at the dentist or doctor's office.

At this point you need to make a Basic Weekly Plan on one of your cards. Write down each day of the week and what your plans are for that day. It is suggested that you plan two days of moderate cleaning, one day of heavy cleaning, one day to run errands and do shopping, one day to be entirely free for yourself and Saturday and Sunday to be free for church and family. This probably sounds too good to be true but it is indeed possible! But it takes, desire, discipline and organization.

The authors of *Sidetracked Home Executives* also suggest making a weekly meal (menu) plan. I'm sure you can see several benefits to this:

1. When you shop you know what to buy.
2. You don't have the 4:00 p.m. panic when you remember you forgot to thaw meat for dinner.
3. You can plan special meals when you have extra time and easy ones (even splurge on paper plates) when it's your "free day."

They emphasize that you did not get into the mess overnight, so you can't expect to get out of it that quickly!

Peggy and Pam suggest a plan for thoroughly cleaning your house—from the inside out! They suggest that you begin at the front door and work clockwise around the house, skipping your kitchen at this point. Put in order every closet, cupboard and drawer in every room until you reach the front door again! You need to put it in your weekly plan and don't try to do every room in one week.

They suggest that in each room, you begin at the door and work clockwise around the room until it is completed; don't get sidetracked into another room! The authors suggest that as you clean, you keep your cards handy and make a list of where everything is. They suggest that you have four boxes or baskets going at one time: 1. Give away 2. Throw away 3. Put away 4. Storage. Their favorite saying is "DARE TO DUMP" it.

They suggest that when the main part of your house is clean, then is the time to tackle the kitchen. After the kitchen, comes storage. They remind you to put storage items in logical places and to keep a record of items in your filebox under "storage" listing their location. You know how it is, if you are not organized, everything you look for will always be in the last place you would have looked for it!

The numbered cards relate to each day. As you make out your weekly plan, put each card behind the date you plan to complete it. Put them in the order you wish to do them in. If you don't complete a task, put it behind the next day, but don't allow this to happen more than three times. If it does, either you don't need to do it or it is something you don't like to do! Pray about it—God will help you!

The authors note that studies prove an act must be done for twenty-one consecutive days to establish a habit, and they suggest that you establish these habits:

1. Put things away when you are through with them. (My husband frequently reminds me of this.)
2. Set the standards for orderliness yourself. (Ouch, that hurts, too!)
3. Never leave the room before closing closets, cupboard doors and drawers (a good habit to teach children).
4. "Pick it up, don't pass it up!"
5. When you fix anything to eat, put away

everything you used before you sit down to eat. (Especially helpful for those who love to cook but hate to clean-up, as I do!)

6. Upon arising in the morning, get dressed, fix your hair, and put shoes on before you begin anything. (The shoes are my downfall.)
7. Never leave the house before you've done all of the everyday duties in the card file box.
8. Check the next day's cards the night before.
9. Finish what you start (another painful reminder).
10. Learn to say "no."
11. Make less promises, but keep them more faithfully.
12. Plan to have a free day; you really need the break and what a satisfying reward! (Far less calories than a hot fudge sundae!)
13. Make Christmas lists early and listen for suggestions. Shopping will be much less hectic and you can save money by picking up things throughout the year when you find them on sale.

Another suggestion is to keep a section for Special Dates to Remember. Could save you some embarrassing situations. Keep a card on file under the 25th to remind you to check to see what special events you should remember next month.

Another important thing is keeping track of where such things as guarantees, special documents, items loaned out, sizes of family members, names of library books and things needed at the store. As the saying goes, "Let your fingers do the walking" and you save a lot of time and energy!

I keep a section of menu ideas plus their recipes.

When making up my weekly plan, I can slip my menu card in to remind me what to prepare for dinner that day. It also helps break the "hamburger" monotony.

Make sure you "plan" time for Bible study and prayer, or there will never be "time" no matter how organized you become!

Granted, this is just a brief overview of their plan and I am in no wise qualified to teach the course they offer, but I hope you were able to glean something of value and that your appetite has been whetted. If you sincerely desire to get your home in order I would suggest that you obtain a copy of the book, or borrow it from the library as I did. If you wish more information you can write or call them at: Sidetracked Home Executives, Inc., P.O. Box 5364, Vancouver, Washington 98668 (206-696-4091).

Certainly this is no "magical cure" for disorganization, but if implemented, can help you become closer to the Virtuous Woman we all desire to emulate!

7
Your "Alone" Time

*T*he query I have heard echoed this past two years is: "He's never at home anymore. He's always at church or out teaching a home Bible study. When he is at home, he is studying for a Bible study! It seems we never see him anymore, and the children, he never has time for them. He doesn't seem to understand and it never seems to bother him. What can I do?"

If you are a minister's wife, or the wife of one who is very active in the church, you have either gone through this, are going through it now, or will go through it! You *will* have an abundance of alone time.

All I can really do with our sisters is to share with them my experience and how the Lord has helped me to oc-cupy this "alone" time, in a positive way rather than a begrudging one.

Brother Putnam and I began dating quite early in our lives, I was nearly fifteen and he was all of sixteen. We dated for three years and then became engaged. During our engagement, he was away at college. We were engaged one and a half years when we received the Holy Ghost at the same prayer meeting. That next year, our last year of college, he returned home, and for one year we went to school together, the first time ever! We were both quite actively involved in campus work as well as the church.

Upon graduation we were married. God saw to it that we remained together, as we both began teaching in the same school. At one point our classrooms were next door to each other. Talk about togetherness! With us, it was a twenty-four hour-a-day experience! We were both still active in campus work, and the Lord allowed us to help out in nursing home ministries. We were *always* together. We even had a three month teaching break in the summer together!

We were always in church together. Both of us had perfect attendance, that is, until May 21, 1975, the date our first child arrived! She was born on a Wednesday, and that first Wednesday began my "alone time!" Often when a couple is very active in church, the separation begins when the children arrive. Mother usually stays home when they are sick, and there are just some places where it is not feasible to take a little one and still be effective doing a work for God. Prisons, nursing homes, small Bible studies, street meetings, and door-to-door evangelism and children, do not usually go together very well!

Brother Putnam began assisting our pastor and was asked to go with him on home visitations and to help out wherever and whenever he was needed. Having the summer off gave him more time to devote to the ministry. I'll never forget one particular incident that is probably typical to other minister's wives: Shortly after our second child was born, I had a severe bout with the flu. I was lying on the couch feeling I would be sick any minute, when my husband walked in to kiss me goodbye. He said that he was going with our pastor to "visit the sick!" (Believe me, he didn't need to go far to find some!)

When we were first married, as we were always together, I enjoyed any little snatch of time I had to myself. I always seemed to have some project going and I tried to do my sewing when he wasn't there. As the children arrived, and the "alone time" increased there were many times when I did feel slighted. At that time he was involved in prison ministry, teaching a home Bible study, announcing for our church's radio broadcast, holding services at a local university, and participating in our local church's drama during the Christmas season. He was gone so much of the time that when he did have a free evening or day at home, he wanted to stay there and rest. I would feel that I had been home long enough and I wanted to get out and do something. I really got to feeling that all we did together was to go to church!

There were probably some times that I could have gotten a babysitter to watch the children so that I could accompany him. As a working mother though, I felt that at least one of us needed to spend the evenings with our children as they were with a babysitter every day while we were at school.

Tensions continued to mount until the Lord answered my prayers and allowed me to stop working and stay at home with our children. Then when I thought things would get better they got worse!

I had been praying for over a year that the Lord would make a way, financially, for me to stay at home with my two little ones. Miraculously, as the Lord always does things, the Lord had moved us to another state and allowed my husband to become the Principal of a very fine Christian school. God had indeed intervened and made a way for me to stay home with my children. Within two weeks we had made the move to a very large city and were ready to begin our first phase of "full-time" ministry.

When we left Ohio, our home was for sale, and as we were waiting for it to sell, the church provided us with a 3½ room furnished apartment that overlooked the church.

As I mentioned, my husband and I had taught together in the same school. Each day we met the same people, were involved in basically the same activities and had much in common that we enjoyed sharing with each other.

Within two weeks, all of that had changed! He went to School/Church (as they were in the same building) and I remained in our apartment with the children, in a strange town, and absolutely no sense of direction spiritually or physically!

Satan chose this opportunity to jump in on all fours! "Ha!" he echoed, "You sit at home all day in this apartment with these kids while your husband is out everyday. Not only is he meeting people you have only heard about. He goes out for lunch every day and is really having a great old time while you sit here wasting your time!"

The more I listened, the more depressed I became.

This went on for two weeks. My poor husband would come home from work, weary and worn from trying to learn a new job, trying to get things organized and prepared for the school's opening day and trying to get some "rather well-used buses" in running condition. Instead of encouraging him and listening to his day, I would dump all of my frustrations and anxieties on him.

After listening to and believing Satan's lies for nearly two weeks, the Lord spoke to me. He simply said, "Isn't this what you have been praying for all this long time?"

Talk about a chastising! It was true. I had prayed for fifteen months that the Lord would open the way for me to be home with my little ones! Yet I had allowed Satan to turn my joy (strength) into sorrow and depression.

The first thing I did, was to rebuke Satan in Jesus' name. The next thing was to thank the Lord for showing me what was happening to me, and repent for allowing myself to wallow in self-pity and allowing those anxieties to overwhelm me as they had.

Right then I decided to make some changes. If we can only realize that the decision to change is always the first step to accomplishing the desired change in our lives. I asked myself why I had desired to stay at home in the first place. A very simple question that I thought had answered. I had instead allowed it to be buried beneath my own self-pity.

I had longed to be home to read to my children, to comfort them in times of distress, to fix them nutritional meals, and to teach them about the Lord. I had failed God and my children in so many ways! But I knew it was not too late to make the necessary changes! I began reading to them and taking them to the library. We began having

"Art Class." I tried to get away from the traditional coloring book and crayons. We played school, played games, did Play-doh, finger paints, cut and paste, posters, collages, we even made "stained glass" window hangings. Occasionally we would join Daddy for lunch.

Even more important than doing things with the children, when Daddy was gone, instead of bemoaning his absence, we would have special prayer for him and the Bible Study, meeting or whatever he was involved in at the time. Often this would develop into our own service which God would richly bless!

If you don't have little ones, surely you could use this time to study your Bible (notice I said "study" not read, there is a vast difference). Perhaps you could get involved in some activity that you've desired to do or learn for years. Learning another language, taking piano lessons, teaching yourself to sew or visiting friends and family could certainly fill the void you find. It would be an excellent time to deep clean your house or get organized "mentally" or in your household.

Our attitude is so important in everything we do. If you are going through a difficult time and don't understand why your attitude is as it is, ask God to reveal it to you. Then knowing, you can understand it and change it.

"When I was a child, I spake as a child, . . .but when I became a man, [woman] I put away childish things" (I Corinthians 13:11).

Often it can be the "child" remaining in us that prompts us with self-centered thoughts. Jesus desires that we "put away the childish things," to really have a selfless love. He desires to be the Lord of all the kingdoms of our heart even in our alone times.

I thank the Lord for helping me get my eyes off myself. I also thank Him for loving me enough to tell me what I was doing wrong and helping me to actually enjoy my "alone time."

8

Get Your "Mental House" In Order

*M*any ladies have really taken hold of an idea ex-
pressed in Anne Ortlund's book *Disciplines of the Beautiful
Woman.* She devotes one chapter to keeping and organizing a notebook. I found it just the thing to "get my mental
house in order." No two ladies could have the same
notebook because no two ladies think exactly alike. It is
an avenue that "fits" the person and her lifestyle.

Sister Becky Enis (Missionary wife to the Military
District of Europe and Asia) and I tease each other that
in losing your notebook, you are literally losing your mind!
It is almost like our own little computer, we can forget a
lot of things but it is recorded in our notebook for easy

retrieval!

I would like to share my own personal notebook with you and hopefully portray the benefits of keeping one.

The notebook I use is not the standard size notebook that school children normally use. It measures approximately 6" x 8", which makes it quite mobile. I even made a fancy little corduroy cover for it with handles that match in ecru lace! (Actually I made the cover more for protection than beauty. After dropping my notebook and the rings popping open, I decided I needed to prevent such a mishap from happening again!) I prefer a looseleaf notebook, which makes it possible for me to add to it and subtract from it easily. Reorganization is a cinch. I have my name and phone number on the inside cover, so hopefully, if lost it could be returned. Sister Enis had her briefcase stolen in Holland. Her notebook was inside with her name and address in it. A month later she received a phone call from the Polezi (Police) saying they had found it and would send it to her via train! (Truly the Lord does answer prayer!)

My notebook is divided into sections by colorful plastic dividers. I've decorated it, somewhat, with some of the beautiful stickers that are so popular today. Holly Hobby proudly announces what is in each section.

My first section is "To Do" of course! Here I make notes of things that I need to do, things that if I don't write down I conveniently forget! Mending, sewing, organizing closets, writing Thank You's, answering letters, whatever I need to do. I also use this area to make my lists and organize my priorities. In the back of this section, I keep a list of phone numbers that I might need while out and away from my card file box. This section probably has the greatest turnover of any.

The next section is my "Agenda." Here I have a calendar, one month per page, with space for notes. It is easy to draw up a "calendar frame" and run it off at a copy machine, or they can often be purchased at an office supply store. Here I try to keep abreast of all of the coming events, list who is suppose to do what and when. Being the pastor's wife leaves me with a lot of responsibility. Keeping an accurate and up-to-date calendar certainly helps. Forgetting sandwiches for the children on "my Sunday," could disrupt the entire church service! Keeping six months or so at a time, helps you to plan ahead, get things in the mail on time, and as your memory fails, you can always look back and get the facts.

The next section is my menu/grocery section. I keep a list of all the products that I use. When it comes time to make my grocery list it really helps me to jog my brain! I also designed pages to list my menus for each day. Occasionally I list breakfast and lunch, but usually I only record my choices for dinner. It also helps me to shop for what I really need rather than buying on impulse. A quick look the night before (whether on my card or in my notebook) lets me know what I need to plan for and saves a lot of last minute rush. You know how it is to "forget" to take the meat out—all you have is a one pound frozen glob of hamburger and you "planned" to have five individual patties! I also keep a list of all the meals I make and a special list for desserts. One quick glance through helps me to vary my menu a bit. I also make special plans for "company" meals. I make a list of all the items I plan to prepare and double-check it as I put it on the table. I've forgotten too many dishes in my time! The experts sug-

71

gest that after your special meal you jot down some important things that can help you plan and prepare for the next gathering.

Next comes prayer. I've made a list of all of the saints in our church, as I pray, I can really remember them and special needs or requests that they have. This is where I write my own personal prayers. I try to date them, it really is a boost to your faith when you realize how completely God answers our every request. Here I have also included some of the pages from the Spiritual Adventure Notebook printed by the Youth Department. They have an excellent section on prayer.

The next section is "Church" and here are notes involving our Ladies' meetings, a list of all of the officers in the Ladies' Auxiliary and their responsibilities. I also keep a list of activities found "tried and true" for our Youth Service and who I have asked to do what activity. This helps to spread the activities to more than a select few who would otherwise automatically come to mind.

Next is my Bible Study Section. I have a page that I got from the Spiritual Adventure Notebook that lists every book of the Bible, it is especially nice to cross off the books as I read through my B.R.E.A.D. program. Also, I keep my own personal studies here. Often questions arise concerning Bible issues and it is important that we search out the answers for ourselves. I wanted to know for myself why it is that we don't believe that women should cut their hair. A word study revealed more than the Scriptures say on the surface and now I understand it "for myself." After all, I'm the one who has to answer to God for me!

I also keep a section to take notes from current reading material. This spring I was asked to speak at a

Ladies' retreat and I used notes taken from a book that I read over ten years ago! If Ruth had had a hole in her apron, she wouldn't have been able to glean very much. I know my memory has a lot of holes in it, so I take a lot of notes.

The section designated with light gray, is for work. I substitute at the local high school and have found it extremely beneficial to make a couple of notes each day about the classes, what they teach, when their planning period is plus whether it was a full day or half-day. It helps too when payday arrives and there is a discrepancy. At one glance I know how to dress, and what problems I may face, I also know which ones to say no to!

Next is my red section—budget of course! Brother Putnam keeps the total budget, but I have a certain amount of money that is mine to budget for food, laundry expenses, and however far I can stretch it. I found that writing every purchase down magically makes it go further, probably because I am more conscious of where it goes! That little extra effort seems to do wonders. It takes some discipline, but I have found it is worth every penny of it.

The next section is where this book evolved from. At first they were just rambling thoughts that seemed to take hold and form into something a little more organized, thanks to a lot of help from the Lord! This section is where I put thoughts that will hopefully develop into something of value at some later date.

The bright yellow section is for messages and sermons. I date them, list the speaker, location, title, Scriptures, and points the speaker shares with us. It is really a blessing to see how God has fitly joined His Word together. Oftentimes the notes from Sunday school will be the beginning of Brother Putnam's message, he of course not knowing it because he was teaching Sunday school in another area of the church. I find I remember much better if it goes through my mode of writing first!

The next section is ME! A semi-journal where I note happenings of the day, poems I like, Scriptures that I need to grow on, Miracles In My Life!, and very personal letters to God (who would search through twelve sections to find this hidden part of me?)

The next section is notes on gifts for my family. Things I plan to make or buy and little hints that they have subtly or not so subtly given me. You can save a considerable amount of money and last minute "I can't think of a thing they want" worries. Write it down, keep it fresh in your mind, pray about it and the Lord will direct you to the sale table it is on!

The last section is the "catch all." I have to be careful it doesn't become a "free for all!" It is all too easy to flip back to all of that blank paper and begin writing only to have to reorganize it all later.

"What do you do when you have 3,000 pieces of paper in your notebook?" I can hear you say. Easy, you file them! "But I don't have a filing cabinet." Make one! You can make a magnificent filing cabinet. All you need is a box, some manila folders (perhaps a business will give you some used ones) and whatever color, style or design of contact paper that fits your color scheme. Cover your box, label your sections, and you are in business! My "file box" is an extension of my notebook. Instead of letting coupons, catalog orders, recipes I've clipped, letters I've received, craft ideas I've run across, mount up and get shuffled from counter to drawer to pile after pile—I have a special manila folder for each. I allow myself one miscellaneous folder, to make sure I don't end up with one entire box marked Miscellaneous and end up in the same condition I began!

Hopefully I have given you a springboard of ideas. Every woman is a unique individual in her own right and has varying needs according to her uniqueness. Allow your notebook to be a reflection and extension of yourself. Used in conjunction with the chapter "Capture Your Vapour" it could change your lifestyle!

9
Too Close
For Comfort

We know, through careful study of the Scriptures, that the visible "Body of Christ" today, is the church. We are baptized into one body, fitly joined together and yet members in particular. God has designed particular aspects and duties throughout His body that we are to perform. We are individuals that come from every station and walk of life and yet through His Spirit, are put together in such a miraculous order that each is able to perform his duties to the perfecting of the Bride of Christ.

Not only are we the "Body of Christ," but we are also considered to be a family—brothers and sisters because of our faith in Christ Jesus.

"For ye are all the children of God by faith in Christ Jesus" (Galatians 3:26).

All of us are familiar with the family structure. As a family we are in very close contact with each other. We eat, sleep and work with the same familiar group for years on end. They know our positive attributes and our negative ones. They know what pleases us, if they've taken time to study us, and they *always* know what upsets us! They see us in our good moods and bad moods. We, in turn, enjoy their good points and tolerate their bad ones! We know that if we don't work together, encourage and uplift each other, that depression, anxiety and stress can do irreparable damage to a family. Problems do arise, but if we try to be sensitive to the feelings of the other members, we can usually arrive at some solution.

As mothers, we try to be keenly aware of our children and be sensitive to their needs. They often go through stages and processes of development that if we did not control our emotions and attitudes, we could severely damage future development of the child and our relationship to him or her.

Take for example a child that is not overly loving and affectionate as the others. Perhaps he appears selfish, doesn't share and causes most of the disagreements. If you don't keep the right attitude and maintain that consistent love, the devil could creep in and tell you that you don't really love that child. In your heart you've unconsciously cast him out and rejected him through no fault of his own. Instead of helping the child through that very difficult period of time with extra attention, love and forbearance, you've given him an outward rejection which is quite possibly what he is experiencing inwardly and has created the difficulty in the first place.

I wonder how often, as a spiritual mother, we react the same way to our spiritual babes. Perhaps we are more demanding and less sensitive to the needs of babes in Christ than we should be. Perhaps we're not tolerant with them and the time it takes for them to develop. Perhaps we feel they are ready for "meat and potatoes" (instruction and reproof) when they are still on the milk.

How about our relationship with our husband? Before we were married we knew we loved him. We thought him to be the most perfect man we had ever laid eyes on! Certainly we didn't dream that when he got up in the morning his breath would stink, and that when he showered, he would leave a trail of dirty clothes for you to pick up!

Hopefully your love for your family has helped you to accept these habits or quirks, and you all live together in mutual harmony.

Often in the "family of God"—the church these quirks or habits set the stage for heartache, bitterness and outright rebellion when saints have gotten "too close for comfort" and have not allowed God to rule supreme in their lives. "How can this happen?" you ask. Although we are a "family" none of us are perfected yet! We are still waiting for that glorified body that God has promised upon His returning. We need to maintain the highest of standards or "the little foxes" will most surely devour the vine.

Thompson, in his "Comprehensive Bible Helps" lists these "social sins" and, if we are not careful, they can be found in the church: adultery, arrogance, backbiting, busybodies, bribery, covetousness, deceit, dishonesty, injustice, neglect of mercy, partiality, the poor despised, pride, selfishness, slander, unjust gain.

Adultery? Oh no, not in the church! Oh, yes. Saints with unsaved mates often seek or find comfort from each other, and if not controlled can fall into adultery. There are even situations where saints who are married to unbelievers believe that it is "God's will" for them to divorce and marry another saint so they can have a "real" Christian home. Matthew 19:9 "And I say unto you, Whosoever shall put away his wife, except it be for fornication, and shall marry another, committeth adultery: and whoso marrieth her which is put away doth commit adultery."

Arrogance. You've seen it. "She'll have to speak to me first, after all, I spoke first the last time." "She walked right past me and didn't even shake *my* hand." Often this attitude builds walls and cliques. God has much to say about it. Proverbs 8:13 "The fear of the LORD is to hate evil: pride, and arrogancy, and the evil way, and the froward mouth, do I hate."

Backbiting. More of this goes on than anyone would like to admit. Often it results in "fried, poached, boiled or roasted pastor" at one or several meals. Can you imagine the effects on young people who felt the pastor was some-one to be respected because of the call of God on his life? More often than not, it does irreversible damage. You've seen people who have grown up in the church and no longer desire to have any part in it. Usually it was because they saw all of the problems and very few of the solutions—namely prayer! Psalm 15:3-5 gives a promise to the one that does not backbite: "He that backbiteth not with his tongue. . .shall never be moved."

Busybodies. We might call them "radar ears" today! They know (or claim to know) everything about everybody and make it their personal responsiblity to let everyone else know too! "And withal they learn to be idle, wandering about from house to house; and not only idle, but tattlers also and busybodies, speaking things which they ought not" (I Timothy 5:13).

Covetousness. You've seen the way the "car bug" or "new house bug" seems to hit everyone at the same time! Or how no one can get anything new but what someone else has to get something bigger and better. "And they come unto thee as the people cometh, and they sit before thee as my people, and they hear thy words, but they will not do them: for with their mouth they shew much love, but their heart goeth after their covetousness" (Ezekiel 33:31).

Deceit. "I probably shouldn't tell you this, but you need to pray for _____ about _____ . . ." Telling "just enough" and leaving "just enough" unsaid to make things appear in your favor.

Dishonesty. Perhaps in paying tithes? After all, how will the pastor know? Remember Ananias and Sapphira tried the same thing. (See Acts 5.)

Injustice. Not knowing everything you think you know and making value judgments on them. "Judge not that ye be not judged" (Matthew 7:1).

Neglect of mercy. The old "they made their bed, now they can lie in it" attitude. "Because that he remembered not to show mercy, but persecuted the poor and needy man, that he might even slay the broken in heart" (Psalm 109:16).

Partiality. "I charge thee before God, and the Lord Jesus Christ, and the elect angels, that thou observe these things without preferring one before another, doing nothing

81

by partiality" (I Timothy 5:21).

The Poor Despised. "Blessed is he that considereth the poor: the LORD will deliver him in time of trouble" (Psalm 41:1). "But Lord, certainly you don't want me to make friends with them. I can't even shake their hand, they stink!"

Pride. "Brother Pastor didn't ask me to sing again to-day. Everyone knows Sister So-and-So is not the singer I am!" "Pride goeth before destruction and an haughty spirit before a fall" (Proverbs 16:18).

Selfishness. "Well, I'd like to help but I need help as bad as they do!" "Even as I please all men in all things, not seeking mine own profit, but the profit of many, that they may be saved" (I Corinthians 10:33).

Slander. "He that hideth hatred with lying lips, and he that uttereth a slander is a fool" (Proverbs 10:18).

Unjust gain. How often do we expect our brothers and sisters to do things for us that we would never think of asking anyone in the world to do for free? A kind sister says she'll hem our skirt. You take her your year's mending and alterations, plus you remembered the fabric and pattern you purchased but never had time to complete! She is expecting a skirt and you bring her "three bags full." How about the cake you ordered for your son's birthday? What bakery would you ever walk out of without substantially reimbursing them for their time, talents and labor? What can be worse? Offering to pay and then not! "Woe unto him. . .that useth his neighbour's service without wages" (Jeremiah 22:13). "At his day thou shalt give him his hire, neither shall the sun go down upon it; for he is poor, and setteth his heart upon it: lest he cry against thee unto the LORD, and it be sin unto thee" (Deuteronomy 24:15). If anything, we should be more generous with our brothers and sisters!

We need to be close to our brothers and sisters, but we have to be careful that we do not become lax and allow the previously mentioned sins to creep into our relationship. All of these "social sins" can be in the church if we fail to maintain the proper relationship with God.

It all begins when we take our eyes off the Lord and begin putting them on man. We will find faults and weaknesses in everyone when we look for them. Let God be the judge.

I admonish all of us to "Keep our eyes upon Jesus."

"And now, little children, abide in him; that, when he shall appear, we may have confidence, and not be ashamed before him at his coming" *(I John 2:28).*

10
Spiritual Abortion And Crib Death

*A*s Christians we all refer to I Corinthians as the love chapter. We quote it at weddings, we use it in marriage seminars, we teach it in our doctrine and hopefully show it to everyone through our lifestyle. We expound on it, applying it to all areas of our Christian walk. I too would like to look at it in the light that we *should* be sharing it with everyone we come in contact with, not just our physical and spiritual family.

I Corinthians 13:4-6 tells us "charity suffereth long." Charity (meaning love) "is kind"—to family, fellow saints, and the unsaved. "Envieth not"—does not desire what the others have. "Vaunteth not itself"—is not proud or boastful.

"Seeketh not her own"—is not selfish. "Is not easily pro-voked"—does not get upset easily. "Thinketh no evil"—does not try to figure out if the rumors about someone are true, always trying to put two and two together. "Re-joiceth not in iniquity"—does not laugh at or scorn a per-son who has had problems of sin or backslidden. "But re-joiceth in the truth, beareth all things, believeth all things, hopeth all things, endureth all things." Charity never (never, never) fails.

What then does this oration on charity have to do with the title of this chapter? Charity, we all know, means love, God's perfect love, but it seems that in certain situations we forget the profound effect that the deep, sincere, love of God can have on a person.

We as divine creations of God, do not believe in abor-tions. We believe that at the moment of conception, a human being exists and we find Scriptures that wholeheart-edly agree and support our belief. I know that with my first pregnancy, one of my greatest fears was that of losing the baby, and having a miscarriage (medically termed abor-tion). Those who have experienced a miscarriage, know the anxiety and heartache it brings. We are surprised to read statistics that report such a high percentage of miscar-riages today, despite the many medical advances and technology of the eighties.

Another very real fear of a new mother is that of "crib death." Medically they have tried to find the cause of "crib death" and tried to pinpoint the babies who are most susceptible to it, but all with little success. They have found that an abundance of protein in the system may be a con-tributing factor.

With my first child that fear constantly hounded me.

She was the type of baby that would sleep twelve hours and stay awake twelve hours. Many, many times when it came time to nurse and my baby was not awake, I would find myself checking on her every fifteen minutes or so, sometimes for hours. I sincerely cannot imagine the grief and anguish of the mother who has lost a baby in this most elusive manner. The guilt, personal incriminations, and loss would be overwhelming if not allowed to be soothed by the Lover of our soul.

We know the church is the Bride of Christ—His chosen bride, which is to be presented to the Almighty God without spot or wrinkle on that greatest of reunion days! The Church is also the spiritual mother of all of the saints. It is hard to believe that in such carefully nurtured surroundings that such things as abortion and crib death could exist, but it does. Oh, how often I have seen it!

I wonder how often the seed has been planted as Paul instructed us to do, and as the tiniest shoot emerged, it was rudely plucked up and tossed aside!

When we are able to witness to someone, sharing with them, not only what God has done for us, but that scripturally the promise is for them too, "conception" has taken place. The developing process has begun, that first spark of life has been born. David tells us that God knew him when he was yet in his mother's womb. Indeed, God knows also that one who is yet in the womb of the Church.

Usually the next step is to invite them to church. Perhaps they have an unfullfilled desire and are searching for truth. They hear the Word preached, and the seed is watered. About the time a root is ready to spring forth and take hold of the truth, some dear saint that has been "in the way" (probably in more ways than one) for quite some

87

time, lets the newcomer know that they would get the Holy Ghost much sooner if they would take that junk off their face, quit cutting their hair, get rid of their TV, quit playing rock music, or whatever other mote he could find to take out of their eyes!

If the Spirit of God isn't completely "overshadowing" that young convert who is seeking the Holy Ghost, the process of "labor" might very well begin! The comfortable, encouraging environment in the house of God that they had begun to desire, is now a thornbed to be shunned!

One dear sister had witnessed to a woman in her apartment building. She was really hungry for God. She had seen many discrepancies in her denominational church and really felt God had more for her. She went to one of our churches with the desire in her heart to be baptized in Jesus' name. She had slacks on at the time. The layman in charge did not find something appropriate for her to wear. But he began to give her a lecture stating that she could not be baptized at all, because if she didn't stop wearing slacks it would defile her baptism, so they refused to baptize her. What happened? Her soul was aborted! Was the love chapter really shown to this hungry woman?

"Crib Death" is another unfortunate occurrence in the church. We all know that babies are not born with the ability to eat meat and vegetables and yet we often try to force feed young "babes in Christ" with meat that they are not spiritually prepared to digest. As I noted earlier, studies show that an unusually high content of protein is found in babies that have suffered from crib death. Do you notice the similarities? This protein causes a stroke in the frail body of a baby because it is too much for the baby to digest. Perhaps this is why God instructed us through Paul:

"Feed the new babes on the sincere milk of the word!"

Babies are not full grown at their moment of birth. Human babies, of all of God's vast creation, take the longest amount of time to reach their maximum size. They are infinitely dependent on their parents for their every need. They need more than physical care from their parents, they need love. Not a superficial love, but a deep, caring love. New converts are no different. In the church we call it "discipling," a lost art to many Christians. We can't just "win a soul" to Christ and then drop them like a hot potato, we have a responsiblity to help them to grow.

We also find that babies do not grow and develop at the same rate of growth. I never envied the mothers whose babies walked at seven months. Thirteen months was soon enough for mine! New converts are the same. We had a new young convert who had a very deep commitment to God and was very sensitive to the Spirit. She came to me one day to ask if God would be speaking to her about her dress, makeup and jewelry. I assured her that He would when she was ready for it, apparently He felt she was ready for it, because He was dealing with her about several things. When they come asking for such advice, that is when they are really ready.

I often think of the love and wisdom my first pastor had for me. When I first received the Holy Ghost, my hair was platinum in color, a far cry from my natural mousey brown! Yet he never said a word to me! I remember sharing with a minister's wife some strange feelings I had been having. I had a habit of wearing a thin gold chain with a small pendant on it. All of a sudden, when I put it on it felt really strange to me. I asked her why she was laughing, she told me that she had been praying that God would deal with me about my necklaces. My next question was, "What else have you been praying about?" I knew there must have been more!

One incident that stands out in my mind involved a young man who had been won to the Lord through Campus Ministry. He had received the Holy Ghost on campus during one of the meetings, and was baptized in our home church. He hadn't had the Holy Ghost long when we took him to a Youth Rally in our area; we felt it would be good for him to meet some other young people and enjoy the worship service. Paul was a typical college student whose uniform was blue jeans and a T-shirt, and as that was all he had, that is what he wore to the rally. He seemed to enjoy the service. He went up to pray at the altar call, and I believe he was really touched by the Spirit of God. After service he went to the back of the church. When he returned to our seat, we knew something had happened. His whole countenance had changed. He never would tell us what had happened, but another saint had witnessed the situation and told us about it. Sister Who-knows-who, took it upon herself to give him a good raking over the coals because he had an American Flag patch sewed to the back pocket of his jeans. I'm sure she thought in her heart that she was doing right, but that was the last time we ever saw Paul. His spirit had been mortally wounded and he died an excruciating death.

Babies need time to grow, they will make mistakes, their "manners" are not the greatest and their choice of clothes may be atrocious. (I know, my four-year-old dressed my two-year-old the other day—navy and white striped top, light blue flowered jumper!) But we have to be patient and give children time. New saints also need time to grow, they too will make mistakes, their spiritual manners may not be the greatest and oft times their choice of clothing is atrocious. We need not kill them in the process though! Jesus in Matthew 18:6 gave us a clear picture and plenty of warning in dealing with new converts: "But whoso shall offend one of these little ones which believe in me, it were better for him that a millstone were hanged about his neck, and that he were drowned in the depth of the sea." Reading on in that chapter we find some pretty serious consequences that we are liable to when we offend someone.

New converts are tender. They need our love, encouragement and prayers, not our rebukes and chastisements. Nowhere in the Scriptures are we given that liberty!

I teach our sisters that unless they are asked, they should not instruct new converts in the matters of holiness standards. If they feel that they need to talk to them about something, they need to talk to the pastor first and get his opinion and approval. I tell them that the most effective thing they can do is to pray for that brother or sister. I know that changes came about in my life because people were praying for me. Not once did I hear a rebuke or admonition from a saint. They let God do all the talking!

We need that charity we read about in I Corinthians 13 to be shed abroad in our hearts. We need that love that hides a multitude of sins.

11

A Prophetess Is Without Honor In Her Own Country

*W*itnessing to our own family about the life-changing aspects of our new found faith and salvation, is usually the first stumbling block in our desire to walk with God. Usually at the precise moment of receiving the Holy Ghost, our first desire is to share it with our family and friends and see them receive this same glorious experience that God has so graciously given us. How marvelous to see our family baptized in the marvelous name of Jesus! That first moment of our new birth so accelerates us that we know how thrilled everyone is going to be by our taking this all-important step in life!

We rush home, believing everyone will want to hear of this glorious truth that God has revealed to us.

Sometimes it does happen this way, but more often than not we are received much as a child who has a new toy whose novelty will soon wear thin!

I received the Holy Ghost one weekend at a denominational prayer meeting in southern Ohio. The next day I needed to return home and as my car was not operating correctly, I called my grandmother to tell her that I would be late because of the car. Briefly I tried to explain what happened to me. I also told her that I would not be eating as I had decided to fast that day. I'm sure that when she hung up the phone, she thought my brain was frozen (the heater in my car wasn't working) because she proceeded to fix a feast for my homecoming! It was quite a struggle convincing her that I wouldn't die of starvation if I did not eat for a couple of days!

Upon relating to her my experience with God, she became quite concerned about my mental as well as physical well-being. Everything I was trying to share with her, she had been taught against for over seventy years. She decided a talk with our denominational pastor would settle the matter. She invited him over one evening to talk with me. He proceeded to tell me that it was quite impossible for me to have received the baptism of the Holy Ghost, speaking in other tongues because only the twelve apostles received this experience. Unfortunately, I did not know the Scriptures well enough to explain these fallacies to him. All I could do was tell him that I knew I had received the same experience they had on the Day of Pentecost! I was emphatic; I had spoken in tongues! He didn't seem all that concerned but I know he did not believe me. I don't believe he really said much to my grandmother about it.

How sad it is today that some profess that they would rather have their children strung out on heroin or alcohol than have them actively involved in any religion!

Grandma knew that something real had happened to me. She watched me very closely before she realized that if I said I wasn't eating that I didn't. She also noticed that I didn't die of starvation! But far more important, she saw a sincere change in my life. The filth that once flowed from my mouth had stopped. My desires changed, instead of going to the bars I went to church, I desired to read and study the Scriptures, and shared them with her. She became quite curious and would oftentimes look up the Scriptures I had given her to study, but she never allowed her pride to accept anything other than what she had been taught in her traditional church.

One day while reading John 4:1-44 I felt the Lord opened a tidbit of thought up to my understanding. It came to me, that we are like Jesus to our family, loved ones and friends. Actually, as the saying goes, "We *are* all of Jesus that man will ever see, and all of the Bible that some of them will ever read."

Get out your Bible, turn to John 4:1 and read through it with me. Verse four tells us that, "He must needs go through Samaria." When we receive the Holy Ghost we have an urgent, burning need to go to our loved ones. We make conversation with them, as in verse ten, we try to share our experience with Jesus to them and try to reveal to them who God really is. We testify of His living water and the gift that He also has for them.

Verses eleven and twelve finds the Samaritan woman

(our family), rebuking Him. "Well, who do you think you are? Do you think you know more about the Bible than Pastor So-and-so who has been to Bible seminary and has been preaching for thirty years?"

As in verses thirteen and fourteen, we try to explain that this is something different than anything they have ever experienced—something that will satisfy every longing desire of their soul, something that the world and its pseudo religions would never be able to do.

As in verse fifteen, they say, "Sir, give me this living water." But when we tell them that repentance is necessary, they begin making excuses. They may go to one church service. The Lord has dealt with the man of God and he delivers a message that they felt was directed solely to them. They think the whole thing was planned because they don't understand the spiritual discernment that God gives.

As in verse twenty, they fall back on what they have always been taught. They feel (if they believe in God at all) that it does not matter where one worships. "Only believe" is their train of thought.

We try to tell them that they really don't know who they worship. "If they pray to the Father, the Son may be offended and vice versa, and of course they can't forget the Holy Ghost!" We try to explain the importance of worshiping God in spirit and in truth, and that in doing so, they will know who it is they worship (verses twenty-one and twenty-four).

They usually do believe that Jesus is coming back (verse twenty-five) but they take a "wait and see attitude." "Oh, I've been hearing that for years" or "Well I'm still young, I've got plenty of time" or, "Well if you can give me an exact date, I'll make sure I'm ready by then."

Fortunately we are able to win some of them to the Lord, but more often than not, it is not an instant transformation. Reading verse forty-four tells us, "For Jesus himself testified, that a prophet hath no honour in his own country." We know that we, as a "prophetess" (a chosen instrument to accomplish God's purpose) are no better than He that they should accept our testimony freely and without question.

Often, because of this, we become discouraged, frustrated and distraught because they do not believe and receive our teaching. Jesus stops us—He admonishes us in verse 35 to look over the harvest. There are many souls that are "white already to harvest." We need to reap those that are ready. We may reap souls that required no labor of ourselves (verse thirty-eight) and yet others we may labor over for years and yet see no fruit.

A young man in our church began witnessing to another young man and praying for him five years ago. This man in turn, shared what he knew, with another man and began requesting prayer for him. The third man began requesting prayer for the second man but neither of them made a start for God, until about two months ago, when the second man came to church, already knowing the truth and what he needed to do to be saved. The third service he was in, he gave his heart to God and received the Holy Ghost. It was a long time for the ripening process to take place, but God indeed gave the increase and the timing was perfect!

What do we need to do? Plant the seed. We can't be like the little boy who was helping his father plant the corn. He got tired and decided to plant all of his seeds in one little spot. He figured no one would ever know, and it was a while until they did find out. But when they did! We must not concentrate only on winning our own family to God. The field (the world) is ready to harvest. Pray for opportunities to witness; God will send them.

I received the Holy Ghost January 16, 1971, and my immediate prayer was for the salvation of my mother. Our relationship had been a very strained one for two years. I was able to plant some seeds, do a lot of watering (with tears in prayer), but I knew I would never be the one to reap her soul. My prayer was, "Lord send someone to her with the truth, someone she will listen to and receive Your Word from." In October of 1982, I received the most blessed reward I could ever have received—news of my mother being filled with the baptism of the Holy Ghost and also being baptized in Jesus' name!

Paul tells us that some plant, some water, but only God gives the increase. We need to continue being laborers, content to work in the field He has chosen for us, and content with our wages whether we began early in the morning of our lives, at noon, or later in the day!

The Scriptures declare we will reap—*if* we faint not. Now is not the time to faint!

"They that sow in tears shall reap in joy. He that goeth forth and weepeth, bearing precious seed, shall doubtless come again with rejoicing, bringing his sheaves with him" (Psalm 126:5-6).

I may not reap my loved ones and carry that sheaf before the Lord, but my rejoicing over their salvation will be none the less for it!

12

Growing In Money Matters

Another area of our lives that often needs much growth, at least it did for me, is the area of money matters. Perhaps we don't really like discussing these issues in connection with the Lord, but it is important to know that our motives, attitudes and principles are correct in this facet of our lives as well as the more spiritual matters.

Some studies indicate that one of the primary reasons women marry is for financial security. Most women do not get married knowing they will be the sole breadwinner "'til death do you part." If the woman is working, she usually hopes to quit at one point or another, usually timed in connection with having children. Today's society is totally different from that of any previous century. Statistics show that over 50% of all women, work today, and 43% of all mothers work. This is an astonishing figure that does not look like it will be changing for a long while.

As Christian women, it is extremely important that our attitude in money matters be correctly aligned with the Word of God. Being Christians does not leave us invulnerable to Satan's attacks on the home in financial matters. This could be where he strikes first and hardest. We must be very careful to keep the door of any problem situations closed to him by aligning ourselves with the statues set forth in the Word of God concerning money.

It is true that God desires that we live by faith taking no thought on the morrow, but He also requires that we be wise stewards with the talents He has given us. He does not want us to get so far in debt that "faith" is *all* that can get us out.

My employment began the day I turned sixteen and could legally obtain a "work permit." My meager earnings went first to pay for clothes, personal needs, then later college. I literally lived a "hand to mouth" existence. The money that came in, quickly went out! There was little to save, with college tuition, books, lunches, gas, parking, clothes, gifts, whatever. My fiance thought I did so great with what I had, that upon our marriage, he put me in charge of "keeping the books!" A disaster to say the least!

I could balance the checkbook all right but with my first year's teaching salary and his unemployment, the balance somehow hovered around $00.00 and never seemed to rise! We made sure we paid our tithes, but as some of John's disciples had never heard of the Holy Ghost, "I'd never so much as heard whether there be any budget!"

It wasn't long before we fell into the credit trap, something many young married couples quickly do. Our cars were on their "last legs" (or so my husband said) so we sold them to buy a newer used car. We needed a washer and dryer with a baby on the way and there were so many good buys on the things we needed, that by the end of our third year of marriage, we owed a considerable amount of money: here a little, there a little.

One day, we came to our senses, realized how interest was eroding our financial base then began a serious move to budget our money.

My husband took complete control of our finances, set us up on a detailed budget and admonished me to be very careful with spending, especially until we could get our heads above water again. He jokingly chided me with "Honey, just because we have checks in our book doesn't mean we have money in the bank!" I felt just like a bird that had had its wings clipped! It may have hurt then, but I sincerely thank God for it now!

Developing a budget may seem like an awesome task that is not only impractical, but also unobtainable. However, if you find yourself in a financial situation that you know to be unpleasing to God, it is your responsibility, as His steward, to make the necessary changes to set it aright. A budget can be that all important first step.

There are many good sources of references to help you develop a budget and encourage you to stick with it. If you can overcome your pride, your pastor may be the best person to help you redirect this area of your life. If he feels uncomfortable dealing with such issues, ask him to obtain the materials on budgeting that Brother J. E.

Yonts has written and included *In My Father's House,* Level III Lesson 33.

A budget follows the basic plan of outgo versus income. It is important first of all, to determine the amount of income earned and brought home per month. (Hopefully, if you work, you have overcome the "what I earn is mine and what he earns is ours" syndrome. One that Satan thrives on.)

Next it is important to list, per month, all expenditures. (This is usually an eyeopener, especially if this is the first time you have dared to write it down in black and white. Unfortunately it often comes up red and white!)

The first item on your list should be tithes. Scripture tells us it should be from our "first fruits," meaning, not only should it be the first thing we plan for and pay, but it should be taken from the total earned before anything else is taken out (gross).

(Just a note here. This "issue of tithes" is something that most ministers of the gospel find very difficult to preach or teach on, as it is so closely involved in their well-being. It is, however, a subject that every saint needs to know, understand and participate in to have the promise of Malachi 3:10 "Bring ye all the tithes into the storehouse, that there may be meat in mine house, and prove me now herewith, saith the LORD of hosts, if I will not open you the windows of heaven, and pour you out a blessing, that there shall not be room enough to receive it." It wouldn't hurt for you to read from verse eight to ten.)

Make a list of your expenses monthly for such items as: House payment or rent, house insurance, health insurance (if not taken out of your check by your company), electricity, gas or oil heat, car payment, car insurance, water, sewer, trash pickup, house taxes, missions, telephone, life insurance, or whatever bills you have.

If any of these items such as life insurance, are paid semi-annually (twice a year) or annually (once a year), then you need to find out how much per month should be budgeted to pay them. Example: If your life insurance payment is $136.00 per year, you need to divide $136.00 by twelve to find out how much you need to set aside each month to pay for it. You will find that you need to save $11.33 per month to cover the cost of this bill. Certainly $11.33 looks easier to save than a $136.00 lump sum bill that arrives and you forgot when it was due!

Don't forget to budget for lunches, gasoline, food, and essentials of daily living. If you have personal loans or payments that are being made to various stores and companies, try your very hardest to keep from charging anything else until all current charges are paid off. Many couples who have been caught in the "charge trap" have destroyed their credit cards to keep from falling into the same old routine.

We got into the habit of charging our gasoline, and of course minor car repairs ended up on the bill. The next thing we knew, we owed over $200.00 to one company because we fell into the trap of only paying the minimum payment due, rather than paying off the entire bill per month. This is where companies make their money and unfortunately we lose ours, often through complete ignorance.

Unless you make an unusually large sum of money, you will be shocked to find out the amount you spend every month on your living expenses. But, as the principle of time stated that you would use every minute you allotted

103

for it, so is our income, unfortunately we often go over that limit without realizing it. People always manage to live up to their income and often above it.

As women we have to be careful of impulse buying, buying on impression rather than on need. Many women have fallen into the snare of buying something to lift their spirits. We need to let God be the lifter of our spirits! Many a man's career and reputation have been ruined by the spending habits of their wives. Let your husband's good name be known in the gates for your good monetary habits.

Another thing to be leery of is becoming too dependent upon the wife's income. As we mentioned earlier, most women do not plan on working the rest of their lives, and yet their spending does not reflect this future change of lifestyle.

We purchased a home knowing it would take both of our incomes to pay for and maintain it—a very foolish thing for any young couple. When our second child arrived, I knew my place was at home with my children, but we had placed ourselves in a very precarious financial situation. The Lord is good though! By faith, I resigned my job, not knowing how we would cut a well-planned $25,000.00 per annum budget in less than half. Our God did it for us and I know He can do the same for you. However, it was a lesson that we will never forget—never to be so completely dependent on my salary for living expenses, that we can not survive without it.

Fighting bill collectors and worrying about bad checks or unpaid bills is not suitable for the children of God. Perhaps many marriages would still be intact today had godly principles been employed in money matters.

13

Bloom Where You Are Planted

"Hearken; Behold, there went out a sower to sow: And it came to pass, as he sowed, some fell by the way side, and the fowls of the air came and devoured it up. And some fell on stony ground, where it had not much earth; and immediately it sprang up, because it had no depth of earth: But when the sun was up, it was scorched; and because it had no root, it withered away. And some fell among thorns, and the thorns grew up, and choked it, and it yielded no fruit. And other fell on good ground, and did yield fruit that sprang up and increased; and brought forth, some thirty, and some sixty, and some an hundred" (Mark 4:3-8).

*H*opefully you are planted in that good ground that Jesus spoke of in verse eight of these Scriptures. The question then is, how much have you grown since you were planted? Jesus often typified us as living, growing organisms such as vines, roots and branches, and I was reminded of these Scriptures when a friend gave me a handful of seeds. She told me that they bear a beautiful plant with purple blooms. I appreciated the gift and told her so, but it left me with an interesting challenge.

I really had a choice to make. If I planted them, placed them in dirt that would allow them to die out to themselves, I would be able to enjoy the beauty which lay dormant and hidden inside. If I simply forgot them, or decided not to plant them, letting them remain in the plastic cup they came in, they would never afford me their beauty. I would have forsaken a love gift from a friend and cheated myself out of a special blessing.

How many times have we failed God by not planting the seeds of faith, His Word, and promises in our heart? How often have we neglected to nourish the eternal gifts that He has so graciously and lovingly given to us? How many times have we allowed ourselves to be cheated out of a special blessing?

My next decision was: in what kind of dirt to plant the seeds? Actually I had several choices. I could have thrown them on the end table amongst the dust that lay there. Dust is dirt you know! But as verse four tells us, they would be devoured. The children, in their infinite curiosity, would have picked them up to investigate, or the dust rag could have eventually swept them up and deposited them in the trash basket.

If I put them in a pot filled with stones, they may attempt growth in the shallow dirt found on the stones, but no depth of roots could ever be manifested.

I could have gone to my yard and dug a spadeful of dirt and placed the seeds in that. But as they strove to develop roots, the dandelions and crabgrass would have soon choked them out.

The best possible choice I could have made was to buy potting soil, good dirt, that has been specifically designed for the needs of the plant. Dirt that has no weeds, no rocks and no parasites that could attack the young plant and sap it of its strength. If I took the little extra time to provide the right conditions for the seeds, I would be able to enjoy the beauty of a full-grown plant in time to come.

Planting the seeds would not mean my part was over. If, after planting the seeds, I failed to water and feed them properly, the young plants would soon wither and die, or rot from over watering. In the process I would not only lose the gift of a friend, but I would lose a touch of beauty in my life.

One day another friend gave me some cuttings from her plants. When I first received them, I put them in water. In time, the roots will grow, and they will also need to be placed in dirt. If I allowed them to remain in the water for an extended period of time, they would not die, but neither would they grow. There is a company today that sells plants and containers under this principle. They advertise that you never have to worry about planting them because they never outgrow their pot. Why? The roots spring forth and soon fill the jar or container, but the plant itself will never mature. It remains at the stage of growth it was when cut from the mother plant.

People are like plants in so many ways! However they

107

are capable of making the choices involved in planting, watering and feeding of their own soul.

Some people are like the cutting that is placed in water. They hop from church to church, attending only the evangelistic services. Their roots may grow, but never have anything to cling to. They are swayed by every wave and wind of doctrine to which they have subjected themselves and they never develop into the mature Christian they could be if their roots were firmly planted in good dirt and allowed to grow in the depth of a stable church.

A church that is founded and solid in holiness standards and the biblical doctrine of salvation is to the Christian as dirt is to the plant. Those precious roots need the nutrients which the special dirt provides. The dirt holds the moisture so that it does not evaporate too quickly. The church has the nutrients to feed the soul of every born again child of God.

"I am the living bread which came down, from heaven: if any man eat of this bread, he shall live for ever" (John 6:51).

"And I will give you pastors according to mine heart, which shall feed you with knowledge and understanding" (Jeremiah 3:15).

But how do you expect to be fed if you are not in the house of God? You need to grow in all areas of spirituality, not just in the ones most convenient.

If I allow the cuttings to take root and then plant them in good dirt, give them proper amounts of water, nutrients and sunlight, they will grow rapidly. At some future time I will be able to share my blessings with a friend.

Later the plant may become root-bound. Physically it has reached its capacity. Roots are powerful sources of strength. All of us, at one time or another, have stumbled over a sidewalk that has been broken and dismantled by the root of a tree. Some roots merely crack the clay pot and continue to grow. Often you will find roots that have seeped into the drainage hole which are quite difficult to remove if allowed to grow very large.

Is not the pot or the plant's physical house a type of the church? Oftentimes the church building has grown to its potential. Revival brings many new souls into the church, but in a few months the numbers return to the pre-revival stage. Growth requires space for expansion! At this point, often a new building is needed that can house more people or perhaps outreach ministries are needed to better handle the "root-bound" syndrome. How has your attitude been about church expansion? Have you supported your pastor in his endeavors or have you thwarted his efforts thinking that a broken sidewalk really is not all that bad?

The spider plant gives us a quaint example of a church that has overgrown its flowerpot. The plant's beauty does not really begin until she sends forth her long shoots with delicate white blossoms. These blossoms are later manifested as babies. So, as the church, expands its outreach ministries, new babes are born into the kingdom of God. Until compensation can be made, it might be a little painful living under such crowded conditions, but the pain is well worth the effort!

If we, as a plant, grow in God's Word (the good dirt), we develop seeds or sprouts when we witness to others. We must always bear in mind that as the Scripture admonishes us; some plant, some water, but only God gives the increase.

What a beautiful opportunity God has given us!

The plant that bears the seeds that were given to me, will never know of the beautiful plant that grew from them. Nor will the plant that bore the cuttings ever know what became of them.

Planting seeds is often a difficult task. It takes work to till the physical ground as it takes work to till the ground of a person's heart that it be ready for the "precious seed of salvation."

"He that goeth forth and weepeth, bearing precious seed, shall doubtless come again with rejoicing, bringing his sheaves with him" (Psalm 126:6).

It often takes years and years of travail in prayer before you "come rejoicing, bringing in the sheaves." But you can rest assured that as the plant, we may never know what has become of the seeds we have planted in someone's heart, the God of all the universe and the Creator of all, knows, because He it is that has given the increase!

Plants not only have a growth cycle, but they must also have a dormant time in completing their natural cycle. In order for them to reach their full potential, they must have rest. The bulb of a tulip is taken from the ground in the late spring and is put to rest on a shelf. In the fall it is replanted. It lies in this dormant state throughout the long winter, but in the spring it bursts forth with unmatchable vibrance because it has had the proper rest and care that it requires. To us this may seem foolish. We think that surely the plant would be more beautiful if it just continued in the blooming stage. God warned us that His ways are

110

not our ways and our ways are not His. "To everything there is a purpose" and God has a plan specifically defined to meet every living thing that He created.

I know that in my own life there was a time that I felt was quite dormant. I didn't understand what was happening. I was frustrated. We had been assisting in a rather small church and my talents were used quite frequently. I taught Sunday school, often had a part in Youth Services, and was active in campus ministry, nursing home ministry, and occasionally sang specials with my husband. The Lord led us to another state where we attended a very large church. This was a church with thirty or so ministers and hundreds of persons desiring any opportunity to do a work for God. I really felt that the only thing I was capable of doing there was warming a pew!

One Sunday morning in Sunday school, the Lord ministered to me through a message entitled *Sitting on the Back Burner.* The teacher spoke of the fact that there are times in our lives when God desires us to "stand back," much like the stew that we place on the back burner, turn the heat down low, and allow time for all of the ingredients to cook down, mix the juices together, and come up with that special taste that only a long simmering can accomplish. I knew that God had given that man, that message, for me!

I began looking at myself, searching myself to see what was happening to me during this simmering process of my life. I was actually surprised to find how many things had really grown in my life that I had not even recognized! I discovered that I had been studying the Bible more, reading more Christian books, becoming a better organized housekeeper, learning how to decorate my home

111

without spending a lot of money, learning how to be a thrifty shopper, had time to visit thrift shops and discount stores, and the list goes on and on. All of this learning was taking place during what I had considered as an inactive period!

We read Scripture after Scripture about the blessings that are bestowed on us because we are the children of God. David said that though he was old, he had never seen the righteous forsaken nor His seed begging for bread.

God has planted each of us for a purpose. Allow your roots to grow deep, like a tree that's planted by the river. Don't allow the lackadaisical standards of the world to pluck you out of the Master's garden.

One sister, while stationed in Germany, kept praying that they would return stateside and that her husband would not reenlist in the army so that God could call them to the mission field. After months of this prayer, God spoke to her heart and told her that He had placed her in a mission field and the army was paying for it! Apparently when reading Matthew 13:38 "The field is the world; the good seed are the children of the kingdom" she had never taken it to mean exactly what it says.

God desires that you bloom where He has planted you. If you will allow yourself to, you will be as Aaron's rod that budded. Once it was dead as your life was before you knew the Giver of life; but when Moses laid the rods before the Lord, as we lay our lives before Him, not only did the rod bud, but it *bloomed* and yielded almonds, and all at the same time! A miracle to say the least!

Don't ever be downhearted thinking that God doesn't remember you or where you are. You are there because He planted you there, now BLOOM!